The Story of
An Irish Jet Pilot

The Story of
An Irish Jet Pilot

AIDAN A. QUIGLEY

THE MERCIER PRESS
DUBLIN and CORK

The Mercier Press
4 Bridge Street, Cork
25 Lower Abbey Street, Dublin 1

ISBN 0 85342 467 5

*To my family—in appreciation;
and to all who work in aviation
in Ireland.*

CONTENTS

ACKNOWLEDGEMENTS

By courtesy of the following companies, I was permitted to utilise their technical documentation in the preparation of this book:

Aer Lingus
Aer Rianta
Boeing Commercial Airplane Company
Esso Petroleum Company Ltd
Pratt and Whitney Aircraft.

Brendan McGann, of the Institute of Psychology of Ireland, gave me permission to use his *Psychological Aspects of Transmeridian Flying*, which he prepared for the Irish Airline Pilots Association, and the Irish Airline Navigators Association.

The Air Traffic Control authoritics at Shannon airport supplied me with the data for the chapter on *The Airspace and the Seas of Ireland*; they also provided me with background information and personal reminiscences of the early days of the Irish Air Traffic Control service.

In the chapter *Passengers*, the stories are based on actual incidents from over the years, but I have used fictitious names, none of which has any relevance to living persons.

FLIGHT

Metals rare and metals common,
Debris of space and stellar death,
Fused in conglomoration, congealed lay cooling.
Dust upon dust, lava and decay.

Metals rare and metals common,
Gleaned and fashioned by human hand,
Fused in union, union scientifically controlled.
Wing to body, fin to tail.

Metals rare and metals common,
Once dust of space and doom of star,
Fused now for human flight in fearless heaven.
Aurora of beauty, cloud and sun.

CHAPTER ONE

AFRICAN SAFARI

The cycle of time bodes no harm to the animal—only man, his greed and his pleasure.

We eased the jumbo jet, *Saint Patrick,* up through the overcast night skies of Europe, and during the climb over Germany and Switzerland the towns and cities below identified themselves only as watery patches of gloomy light in the carpet of cloud. Heavy with fuel and eager tourists, the flight was bound from Frankfurt to Nairobi in Kenya.

The initial selected cruising altitude was 29,000 feet, because the aeroplane was too laden to climb to a higher level; by the time we were over Italy enough of the fuel would have been used, and then the plan was to go to 33,000 feet and maintain that height all the way to Kenya.

Soon the German controller's voice was replaced by his Swiss neighbour and then an Italian, until the Mediterranean was almost behind and a voice from Benghazi gave us safe passage over the Libyan desert. The bright stars were there as before and a friendly wind from the African night, but the stars were ignored by the inanimate precision navigation system whose computer brain steered the aeroplane with uncanny accuracy over the wastes of the Sudan. Our guidance equipment was totally self contained, and it required no help, even from the celestial bodies, to navigate over the surface of the earth.

In these regions, air traffic control procedures and communication are not as sophisticated as in Europe, and the voice of the controller at Khartoum was only a crackling of unintelligible jumble on the High Frequency radio. But the great herd of aeroplanes was protecting itself, and the different voices and accents came incisively through the night on a standard frequency:

'All aircraft: this is Speedbird 464, northbound Nairobi to London at Flight Level 350. Position Debadeb at 0200 hours, estimating Bravo November Alpha at 0213.'

'Speedbird 464: this is East African 655—if you are in contact with Khartoum will you please relay a message for me?'

A Nigerian aircraft, bound from Lagos to Mecca in Saudi Arabia, was exchanging his position and height information with Air France who was on a northbound crossing track—Air France climbed up a further 1,000 feet to ensure positive separation. Here was the region in the Sudan where our maps had an overprint which read: DISPLAY LANDING LIGHTS IN THIS AREA.—the reason being that the holy pilgrimage to Mecca, the Hadj, was in full swing, and large numbers of the faithful were flying from the African west coast to the Mohammedan shrine in Saudi Arabia—the track intercepted the main north south air traffic flow at right angles.

A hostess entered the cockpit and said, 'Captain, one of the passengers wants to know why the landing lights are on.'

'Tell him', replied the co-pilot, 'we are on the look out for fellas on flying carpets on their way to Mecca.'

The radar scanner had picked up no weather, but earlier the desert was dotted with the red glow of burning gas from the oil wells; now there was nothing but arid waste, and even the White Nile passed beneath undetected. To the east the sky had lightened in colour and the dawn swept in from the Indian ocean, over the Abyssinian Highlands to the plains of the Sudan. Jumbo purred along unconcernedly, content with gentle headwinds at 33,000 feet and making only a mechanical gesture to the dawn: I had switched off

8

its navigation lights.

Now the night was over, and the magnificent mountains and table lands of Kenya lay ahead; Mount Kenya itself was to the east with a summit that resembled a temple—perhaps this was the residence of that fabled Kikuyu god who supposedly lived on top of the mountain. The temple of the god was 17,000 feet but its grandeur was to some degree diminished by the scale of the ground all about it.

I closed the throttles back, and those engines that had given cruise power for 7 hours idled on the stops in rest, as gravity drew the aeroplane down over the Ngong hills, and I guided it in towards the long runway at Nairobi. Easing up the power to arrest the descent, we lowered the flaps and the undercarriage; a soft rumble of 18 wheels on the concrete and *Saint Patrick* had arrived from Frankfurt.

'Jambo', said the baggage loader, and the customs officer and the crew car driver—to which I replied with a thumbs up sign: 'Yes, jumbo.'

It was only when the waiter at the hotel said: 'Jambo', that I realised that he could not have known that we were connected with jumbo aeroplanes. He explained in perfect English, that 'Jambo' was the Swahili word for 'welcome', and as we discovered, only one of the many rich words from the Swahili tongue that also expresses traditional concepts and lore in delightful proverbs.

After two refreshing cups of Kenyan tea, I said: *Nataka kwenda kulala*. I read it from the handout leaflet, 'I want to go to bed.'

*   *   *

My wife Stephanie is a graceful Irish dancer, and many times I watched in admiration as she hitched up her skirt and twinkled across the floor with her pretty feet tapping out *The Rakes of Mallow*, but now the scene is different in the woods of Kenya, as two Giriama tribesmen beat out the rhythm for the Gonda dance, and a medicine man gyrates

9

his body and his crazy head dress to mesmerise a reluctant
young bride. . .

Beauing, belleing, dancing, drinking,
Breaking windows, cursing, sinking,
Ever raking, never thinking
—Live the Rakes of Mallow.

The voodoo man was not familiar with that song as he
danced his ritual to remove the bewitchment of the maiden.
She now agreed to her marriage and the tempo of the dance
of joy increased, and her four bridesmaids were joined by
the groom. Again the bride became reluctant, and now the
groom performed a symbolic propitiatory dance, but it was
all to no avail, and he has to consult with the medicine man
once more, who gives her certain powerful potions to win
her back. At last the final ceremony is performed and the
couple are serenaded home with a Sengenya song. The
drum beat never faltered in all this time, but throbbed continuously for the graceful sensuous movements of the
dancers.

'Then to end this raking life,
They get sober, take a wife. . .
Four thousand, five hundred miles away in Mallow.

*   *   *

I gripped the steering wheel of the Landrover tightly, as
the rutted ribbed surface of the road through the Masai
Game Reserve pounded the suspension; but yet the rough
ride did not prevent us from marvelling at the surroundings.
The dirt track wound through a parched landscape dotted
with decaying wood and stunted trees, and the occasional
carcass of a wildebeest lay grotesquely in the dust where
lately a pride of lionesses had breakfasted. Now a Masai
warrior raised his spear in greeting; here a family sat under
the shade of a tree near the roadway, dignified in posture,
refined in features and ornate in dress.

A huge mountain commanded the horizon, and its shape

10

resembled Nephin in my County Mayo, but for the fact that a large breast-like extrusion was predominant on one of its slopes.

The heat of the sun was pleasant, and as the track twisted and turned, Nephin appeared in various places, and despite my attention to the steering wheel my mind departed the Masai and their game reserve and drifted back over the years to waving bog cotton, a dusty road, a pedal bicycle, an Irish summer evening and the real Nephin yawning with pleasure as it looked down on Lough Cullin. We zig zagged the bikes across the roads to avoid the ripe cow pads, and stopped to talk to Michael Burke about our new class in the National School.

Soon the road entered the lush woodland with its stunted oak trees, and clusters of insects hovered in the streaked shafts of filtered sunlight; and then the pedals of the bicycle were pumped up and down faster and faster as the calm surface of Cullin appeared tantalisingly through the gaps in the trees. . . 'Hi Skipper—there's Lake Amboseli over the the right.'

In the heat of the plain the African lake shimmered and covered a vast area, with dark black islands looming large upon its surface; but somehow the nearer we got to it the further it receded, until the islands were seen as small hills, and the waters as a mirage with dust devils drifting across their eternal nothingness.

The water hole at the Amboseli lodge was brightly lit at night, and the drinkers took their place there at the salt lick throughout the hours in the ranking of the jungle.

A restless cheetah padded its way around the sleeping huts and a monkey capered on their roofs, but the light came early and the guide had us out amongst the herds of gazelles, but they wound their colourful tails like propellers and bounded away into the dawn; lionesses tried to encircle them but their gracious speed gave them the right to another day of life. Zebras mixed with groups of wildebeest, and a rhino ate in the same grass patch as an elephant

11

and its baby. Buffalo stared with uncomprehending eyes, and their very docility belied their ferocious nature; by the window of the Landrover a lioness played with her cubs, and floppy vultures straddled a tree waiting to pick the carcass of her kill. A leopard ignored us at five feet and rolled over in the sun, whilst close to a water hole the articulated silhouette of a giraffe nibbled at choice leaves from a high tree. . .

'Dublin tower clears EI-ASJ to land; runway in use is 24 with the wind from 270 degrees magnetic at 20 knots—gusting to 30, the runway surface is wet.'

Jumbo clawed its way onto the ground, shuddering in the cross wind and showering up masses of spray as reverse thrust slowed it down.

Jambo; umetoke wapi—'welcome, where did you come from,' said the Irish customs officer.

'Nairobi,' I replied.

CHAPTER TWO

ATLANTIC CROSSING

Ocean waves toss in endless array,
Wild winds are flecking the waters in spray,
But high near the sun with gossamer string,
A jet plane is flying on tranquil wing.'

The captain and his co-pilot reported for briefing one hour before the scheduled time of departure of the flight. The third pilot had gone out to the plane to join the engineers, and to complete his pre-departure and safety inspection. As he walked around the jumbo, the final gallons of kerosene were being pumped in for the first sector—the trip from Dublin to Shannon.

In the briefing room the flight dispatcher laboured at his paper work, and the air around him was vibrant with radio transmissions from departing aircraft, clacking teleprinters and busy telephones. The movement board above his desk displayed the flights that he was handling for that day: Cubana, two Yugoslav aircraft, three Aer Lingus 707's, four Canadian charter DC 8's; in the middle of the postings was the jumbo jet EI-ASJ, with a planned departure time out of Shannon of 1620 hours.

The briefing commenced with an outline of the routes or tracks available over the North Atlantic; earlier that morning the air traffic control authority for the ocean region would have designated these tracks, based on their studies of the weather plot giving the most favourable winds. The tracks had various points of origin: some were overhead Shannon, more were south of Cork and one began at Eagle Island in Co Mayo. There were other flight paths too which were hundreds of miles to the north of Ireland: these would be used by overflying traffic from the Scandinavian countries.

The tracks were referred to as A, B or C etc.; E or Track Echo was the one selected for the Irish Flight 109 because it began at Shannon. Echo then ran to 54 degrees North latitude and 15 West longitude, to 55 North and 20 West, and so by named latitude at each 10 degrees of longitude to overhead Gander in Newfoundland.

The crew studied the weather conditions at Dublin and Shannon, and they reviewed a high level meteorological chart of the North Atlantic, where the dispatcher had transcribed the actual route to New York. The briefing continued with a reference to areas of possible turbulence and a mention of jet stream winds; these are winds of unusual speed at high altitudes that twist their way in narrow bands through the earth's atmosphere.

The flight plan was a computer print-out that had been programmed with winds and temperatures and the aircraft's performance capabilities. Each sector was presented with height, distance and speed, and the amount of fuel to be consumed. The trip time was to be 5 hours, 54 minutes with a calculated fuel consumption of 70 tonnes. The detailed fuel usage was tabulated at the bottom of the sheet, and it revealed that a further 26 tonnes was required for approach procedures, en route discrepancies, and provision for a diversion to Washington should weather conditions deteriorate at New York.

Next, the pilots worked through the mass of teleprinter weather forecasts for the airports along their route down the eastern seaboard of North America. The dispatcher discussed the Equal Time Point which was calculated between Gander in Newfoundland and Shannon. It was the halfway point in time, but not in distance; it was the position where if beyond it, should a serious emergency occur, the flight would have to go on to Gander; before the point the jumbo would return to Shannon. . .

I was hitching a ride, and I strapped myself into the auxiliary seat behind the crew. The co-pilot flew the first leg to Shannon.

* * *

At 1630 hours the jumbo jet set course and climbed out west for its cruising level of 31,000 feet, and in that comfortable aeroplane were 3 pilots, 16 air hostesses and 338 passengers. The radios in the cockpit picked up continuous communications chatter, and in the cabin the hostesses prepared for a busy afternoon. The voice of the air traffic controller, who had given us climb out instructions, was familiar to me, and he was a Mayo man too; we had both flown Hurricanes in the same unit. . .

In 1943, No. 1 Fighter Squadron was stationed in Shannon, and I had the opportunity to fly many times up over the countryside that I loved so well. As a boy, I had not realised that the town of Foxford stood on a plain and thus from the air was difficult to pinpoint. Nephin however, that pyramid-like mountain, caught the eye with its set piece lakes, Conn and Cullin, and drew you towards it. I had pushed the nose of the Hurricane fighter down over Granny Healy's at Pontoon, and then went low over the waters of Cullin. From the railway bridge, where we used to shoot wild geese, the run to Foxford was less than a minute, and I went up steeply at the town and barrel rolled until the repetitive manoeuvre exhausted the climb and I levelled off and looked down in pleasure at the scene below.

The town clung tightly to the banks of the Moy and the woollen mill dominated the picture, and I could see that the river which gave birth to it all, did indeed flow in slow majesty, with generous sweeps and easy grace, along the ten miles to Ballina. But that same river had other moods too, and in winter spate it flooded many of the fields along its banks, and if the farmer was late with his second crop of hay the waters in their overflow would run around the contours of the ground and make islands of the haycocks, and rot them where they lay. The fields and the farms were despoiled by the continual winter inundation; the hungry waters of the river perpetually drained away their very life-blood and deposited it along the banks as muddy waste whilst its substance flowed down to the sea. Some consolation was the fact that the marshy ground was alive with geese and duck.

This part of Mayo was renowned in the past for its poteen, and Glass Island in Lough Conn was a centre for the trade. For the Civic Guards, it was an easy raid as far as access was concerned, but their efforts were usually blighted by the fact that the island was close to the shore road, and thus the approach of the raiding party was under observation from the start. The place is desolate now as all the families who live there have either died out or spread to the mainland. . .

1640 Hours

'Shamrock 109—change to Shannon Area. Squawk A0325 with height read out.'*
The co-pilot set up the frequency on the transponder.

Senior hostess enters the cockpit and says that she is making some nice strong tea for today's important men. I relished the thought as I interested myself in the radio reports.

'Area Control request the Shamrock to report level at 310, and to call passing 220.'

'George Able Yankee Lima Juliet from Bristol Lulsgate—estimating Tuskar Rock at 03.'

---

* The expression 'Squawk. . .' is an instruction to the pilot of an aircraft to transmit a radio signal on a special frequency, for the purpose of radar identification. Height is simultaneously broadcast—automatically.

'Aer Lingus 765 by Clonmel requesting descent.'

'Aer Lingus 765 clear descent to 70. Call leaving 240.'

I knew the pilot of 765, he had flown Lysanders in the Air Corps...

We flew quite frequently as target aircraft for the anti-aircraft batteries. The Ack Ack called the exercise a 'burst short', since their shells, devoid of shrapnel, were fused to explode at a safe height below the Lysander.

I was flying up the Dublin coast on a sunny afternoon, accurately maintaining the desired 10,000 feet for the batteries; the warm sunlight was streaming through the large cockpit windows of the plane, and I was admiring the deepening tan of my left arm which was leisurely draped along the padded rest. The shell bursts were far below but something seemed to have disturbed the fairly steady tempo of the barrage; as we turned back for the last run along the range line I saw a German JU 88 coming in from the east. I knew if he had seen me he would not have gone through the process of closing courteously to identify the markings; a Lysander was a type in common service with the RAF. We quickly sought the refuge of a fat cumulous cloud, and when its misty sanctuary finally expelled us, he was nowhere to be seen.

1646 Hours

'Lufthansa 467 checking receiver on emergency frequency 121.5.'

A small fly, trapped in an alien environment was crawling across the vast windscreen of our jumbo, a screen that is composed of glass laminations over three inches thick. The insect had been there during the cockpit check on the ground, and although the pilots had heard its frantic buzzing, and the interruption when it collided with the glass, they could not locate it to remove it.

How tiny things and inconsequential sounds pluck the strings of the memory. The buzzing sound brought me back to Foxford, and that delightful walk down the Green where the road by the river followed the gracious sweep of the Moy. I used to walk there with my mother of an evening and the grassy banks and the meadows nearby were alive with the sounds of the bees. I visit her grave every summer, in the old cemetery at Craggagh, and the tranquility of that lonely place is a haven for those little creatures searching for honey amongst the wild roses and the mountain flowers that bloom all around.

1649 Hours

Cabin supervisor calls on the cockpit telephone, and ask the third pilot to come down to the first class section and check out the refrigerator at the horse shoe bar.

'GAYLJ Calling Shannon—estimating Tuskar now on the hour.'

Co-pilot of Shamrock 109 reported to Shannon, that EI-ASJ was passing Flight Level 220 (22,000 feet). Shannon acknowledged and asked him to call High Level Control on 135.6.

Lufthansa 467 confirms that his receiver is OK. The German voice is guttural and heavily accentuated...

When World War II was ending, each BBC radio bulletin brought new announcements: 'The Germans in Holland have surrendered and remaining enemy troops in Denmark in contact with Allied Headquarters to arrange immediate capitulation.'

The morning at Gormanston was misty with a drift of fog banks from the sea, and the cloud base was 200 feet as the unmistakable roar of a German bomber thundered across the wakening camp and lost itself to the west where the ceiling was lower, and it had climbed to avoid collision with the rising ground. They made a landing from the fourth sweep: the latest model of the JU 88—a fast truck with a mounted machine gun tore out from the apron to meet the aircraft.

The crew switched the engines off and clambered out of the aeroplane; they were wearing Luftwaffe uniforms with the ugly bum freezer jackets. The pilot, a sergeant major, had facial scars; blue eyed and blond, he looked a tough customer and he wore the Iron Cross; his two companions were corporals, one a gunner, the other a navigator, but neither had the moulded and dedicated look of their pilot.

We eyed them with suspicion as the sergeant major stood in front of our CO and saluted; the German explained to the commandant that Denmark had surrendered, and that his squadron had been given the choice by their commander of flying their machines to neutral countries before the truce was valid. He had decided to come to Ireland, and he recounted, with just a twinkle of Teutonic humour as to how he had flown all the way across England, flat out and very low, gun button safetied, and admired the scenery for the first time.

We gave them breakfast, and then brought them to a guarded barbed wire protected billet, where they remained for a few days before being taken to GHQ for interrogation. High ranking German officers were reputed to be fleeing from Europe in the guise of ordinary flight crew, but our sergeant major and his two crewmen proved to be genuine; they were subsequently interned in the Curragh.

During their stay at Gormanston, I never quite found out what they thought we had in store for them, because they requested permission to run up the engines of the Junkers each morning; we had taken the precaution of pointedly draining off most of the fuel in their presence and removing the armament. The engines had a most unusual sound as they raced them to their peak: they had fuel injection which was unique at that time. The navigation equipment resembled a ticker tape machine, and it rolled out with monotonous precision each day, the exact latitude and longitude of Gormanston Camp.

The inside of a German aircraft smelt rather oddly, and it possibly came from the amount of artificial material that was used in the construction of the interior fittings and the instrumentation. Perhaps the smell was just peculiarly

19

German in the way that the various odours associate themselves with different races. There was a dump of crashed German aircraft at Baldonnel—mostly Heinkels and Junkers, and the air around was heavy with this unusual chemical smell.

Towards the end of the war, our neutral skies were filled with the aircraft of the participating nationalities and many crashed around the countryside. The Germans always managed to set theirs on fire or blow them up, but the British and Americans left their machines intact.

1654 Hours

At 25,000 feet the third pilot adjusted the power to 1.4 engine pressure ratio. The outside air temperature was -30° Centigrade and the speed 366 knots; rate of climb was now 700 feet per minute.

Captain called Shannon with the estimated time of arrival at 54 North and 15 West. He gave a time of 1711 hours as the automatic inertial navigation computer read 17 minutes to the next position.

An Aer Lingus BAC 1-11 is asked to change to Shannon High Level Approach. I recognised the pilot's voice as Hammy's. . .

Captain Ivan B. Hammond was affectionately known to all from general manager to hangar sweeper, as 'Hammy', and he, together with a few other captains from the older school, were our mentors in those early days of primitive navigational aids and morse key radio signals.

Hammy was a self-made aviator and he had come up through the system the hard way: he earned his money at a mediocre job and then handed it over for flying lessons and aviation night school. He flew with Aer Lingus from 1936, and unlike some pilots from those years, Ivan progressed with the newly developing art of blind flying and all that went with it in cockpit instrumentation and radio aid expertise.

He had evolved his flying style in his own way, and if his

20

techniques were different from others, I can never remember him making a bad landing. I sat in the co-pilot's seat of a DC 3 and watched him in strange places seek out radio bearings like a terrier searching for a bone; once he locked on to them he held—whatever the weather. With the wipers pummeling back and forwards across the smeared windows, Ivan would also have his side panel back, peering expectantly into the darkness waiting for the approach lights to come up, as we broke from the low cloud and swept in from the gloom to the landing area.

After the touch down was completed and we bumped across the grass to the apron, I would hear—'OK, you can take her back to Dublin, Sonny.'

There were others like him who taught us the job of being airline pilots, helping us to gain confidence with our limited experience of bad weather—making an approach to an airfield on a foggy morning, when the only way to get in there was to fly across a marker buoy on the estuary beneath, and hold the heading until the glasshouses on the far bank heralded the runway coming up. We ignored the turbulence and the icing and obtaining a fix of position on the magical Gee box, exercised our academic knowledge of navigation using poor aids to establish a position and an estimated time of arrival at the destination airport.

Much of the early aircraft position fixing was by the use of wireless telegraphy bearings received by a radio officer from a ground station. Some of our operators preferred to use a 'bug key', which sent the code out at a fast speed but was inclined to clip the sound of the notes; on one memorable day as we flew towards Northolt, an exasperated operator at Uxbridge signalled my bug operator: 'Send with the other foot'.

1658 Hours

Alitalia 649 reported squawking A0322 at Flight Level 310. He was estimating Lee at 1706; Cork was his next position.

Shannon replied: 'After Cork clear to proceed direct to 54 degrees North and 15 degrees West.'

A Swissair 747 asked for permission to remain at Flight Level 310 for a further 10 minutes as he was too heavy for 350.

The co-pilot undid his safety harness and said to the captain: 'OK Skipper if I go aft for a pee?'

He is a great man for dry jokes; he established his reputation many years ago when he asked a multi-chinned business executive if he had to use a book marker when he was having his breakfast.

There were two Uncle Franks in my family: one was a traveller with the woollen mills, and he was without doubt the best storyteller in the west of Ireland; the other was a fireman on the airport tender, and although I had not spoken to him for years before the incident, I welcomed his anxious face peering in at me through the side window of a wounded DC 3, a long time ago.

This flight was taking off for Paris, and was but a short distance down the runway, when the co-pilot mistook something that I had said to be a command to retract the undercarriage—he pulled the lever. Such an accidental selection could not occur in a modern aeroplane, because an interference mechanism, operated by switches that sense the weight at the trucks, physically prevents a premature retraction whilst the machine is on the ground. The gear came up, unexpectedly to me, and the DC 3 sagged slowly to its knees and graunched to a halt along the concrete. The propellers bit into the runway and bent backwards; there was no fire and little damage except to the propellers themselves, nobody had panicked and there were no injuries—but there was my humiliation and Uncle Frank's helmeted face anxiously peering in at me through the windscreen.

The older Uncle Frank had very expressive hands, and a ritual was always involved in the way in which he lit a cigarette and removed it from his mouth. Very positively up and back went the head, in went the cigarette and so it was lit.

22

The removal required, first of all, the full distention of the fingers of the right hand before they ever reached the face, then with slow ceremony the palm went flat on the side of the cheek, and the fingers squeezed together with equal panache to gather the fag—now was the danger time, that's if you didn't know Uncle Frank. He carefully transferred the cigarette to his left hand, and the palm of the right smote you with some force on the chest—now you were off on the story.

1700 Hours

'Shannon, Saturn 955—Flight Level 370, estimating Cork at 1724 hours.'

'Saturn 955, expect Flight Level 410, sqawk A0331.'

'Alitalia 640 requesting High Frequencies in use?'

'Alitalia 640—you are on the wrong frequency, call Shanwick on 127.9.'

'Saturn 955, this is Shannon, I am not receiving your transponder, squawk now A0367. . .'

I flew Hawker Hind 67 for the first time in May 1941. The Hind had been intended for two roles: a trainer and a medium day bomber; it had outlived its usefulness as a bomber, but it was an excellent trainer and was engined with a powerful Rolls Royce Kestrel. The aeroplane was one of a long line of Hawker biplanes that culminated in that famous monoplane fighter of Battle of Britain drama, the Hurricane.

The wings and the body of the Hind were constructed with formers of tubular metal, upon which linen fabric was stretched tightly, stitched in position, and then sprayed with special cellulose dope; both wings and the tailplane were braced with strong wires and stays. There was a rear cockpit from which an observer could fire a Lewis machine gun.

Despite the aeroplane's deficiences, the Air Corps used it for dive bombing exercises with small smoke bombs suspended from racks beneath each wing. It was impossible to manoeuvre the machine into anything resembling a steep

23

diving angle, but yet the engine went into a diabolical sounding whine, the slipstream almost tore the goggles from the face, and the pilot was left wondering when the fabric was going to shred from the wings or their very structure collapse from the strain of the attack.

In the terrifying dive you glued your eyes to the long tubular Aldis sight, and it was easy to imagine that the tar barrel on the water below was terrified too, because it kept weaving back and forward across the sight glass. Your right hand was tugging and yanking an ancient lever, which through a system of gates, like an old gear shift, eventually conveyed its movement to the bomb release mechanism under the wing. The target was safe from me, because most of the bombs fell hundreds of yards away, and the last one tumbled down near the observation post as I flew over it for the subsequent landing.

1703 Hours

Captain picks up microphone and reports to Shannon: 'Level at 310, speed Mach .84.'
Control replied: 'Roger, call again at 15 West.'

1704 Hours

'Swissair 168—over Cork at Flight Level 310, can now accept 350.'
'Swissair 168—report leaving 310. Be advised Swissair 168—aircraft reported light to moderate turbulence on your track to 15 West at Flight Level 350.'

1706 Hours

TWA Reports light chop—light turbulence at 350.

1708 Hours

'Shannon—this is Air France 017 at Flight Level 310, estimating Cork at 1724.'
'Air France 017, squawk A0336 and report Cork. Clear 340 on Delta track.'

The co-pilot had slid the green glare shield across the windscreen to protect his eyes against the sun, and the shiny surface of the perspex mirrowed my face in an odd far away reflection. I was a boy once again, sitting on a half cut turf bank on a summer's day and gazing down into the still waters of a bog pool; I bobbed my head around and a small face moved amongst the reflection of little puffy clouds and a bright blue sky. Now and then the image was rippled by a water beetle zig zagging across the blue panorama; it disappeared among the reeds and then scurried out again from a different direction, and I wondered if it was the same insect. I threw in little pieces of turf, and the blue sky with the small face and the white clouds see-sawed up and down, until all was still once more and other water beetles appeared and scuttled about like their companion.

My chum called me, but I snuggled further down into the heather and lay still and listened to the bees. 'Come on,' he shouted, 'the float is wating for us, and we have to bring the can of tea and the sandwiches down to the men in the meadow.'

When we got there Willie Kennedy gave us a puff from his clay pipe.

1711 Hours

Co-pilot reports: 'Shamrock 109 by 15 West at Flight Level 310 and estimating 55 North and 20 West at 1738.'

Shannon told him to change to Shanwick on 127.9 and request his High Frequency assignment.

The third pilot logged the fuel readings and made an adjustment to the engine power.

1713 Hours

Captain dials PA-PA on the cabin public address system and then speaks to the passengers. As he does so the co-pilot starts singing a bawdy ballad; captain digs him across the cockpit with his elbow and continues talking into the telephone.

1717 Hours

Crew saw a contrail up ahead: it was from another aeroplane, and its blip was painting on their radar screen at a distance of 30 miles. Soon the contrail disappeared, but a little glistening silver dot remained in the clear blue sky.

1720 Hours

Hostess comes into the cockpit and reports that it is too warm in Zone 2. She asks the third pilot for a cigarette and then says that a passenger, who insists he has permission to visit the cockpit, is making a bloody nuisance of himself since they left Shannon. Captain says: 'Keep the nut in the cabin.'

'I like your new uniform, Maura,' remarked the captain. 'Bloody gorgeous,' said Frank, 'you were like a crowd of green fairies in the tights. . . '

The first handmade suit that I ever wore was in 1940, and it was the uniform of an officer of the Irish Army. It was tailored in Dublin by an old firm of military outfitters, who for many years had catered for the needs of the British garrisons in Ireland. It seemed strange though that at that time, in 1940, some of their uniforms still on the stocks were of the formal type, with scarlets and blues and embroidered gold epaulettes; they were obviously intended for peace time functions.

The elderly cutter had this in mind as he measured me for a pair of Bedford cord breeches—these were worn for ceremonial purposes. He recalled, that just as some of the soldiers in the early stages of the Boer war were easy targets in their red tunics, young medicals from Dublin were commissioned in World War I, and sent to Flanders in light coloured breeches. 'They were picked off,' said the cutter, 'by German soldiers wearing glasses.' He had made the breeches, but some of the young officers were dead in France before they could pay the tailor.

1741 Hours

Position 55 North and 20 West—three minutes late; speed is 404 knots, windspeed reads 100 knots from a direction of 245 degrees true.

Third pilot again jots down instrument readings and notes the postion of the engine throttles.

More tea arrives in the cockpit.

1750 Hours

Co-pilot listens to Canadian weather broadcasts, and writes down the forecasts and the actuals for Gander, Goose and Montreal.

'Did you hear that, Skipper?' — Frank removed his earphones and continued: 'Temperature at Montreal is 33, and snowing heavily. Gander has ice on the runways with braking action reported as fair. That's a bit early for that sort of jazz don't you think? . . .'

Many of the winters at Foxford used to bring a heavy frost, and the flooded fields above the town provided an admirable skating rink. There were a few sets of skates, so most people made their fun by resorting to the local method of sliding along the ice. It was essential to wear a pair of heavy books with soles well studded with flat headed cobbler's nails. A brush handle, spiked at the end with a long nail, and stroked like a canoe paddle, propelled the wielder along the ice at a modest speed.

1810 Hours

'This is New York with terminal forecasts for period ending 0200 hours.' Frank logged it down.

1827 Hours

Position 55 North and 30 West passed to Gander Radio.

Hostess with the shapely legs brings in four cups of clear soup.

Neat cardboard folder, which the third pilot had prepared for crew to monitor fuel burn-off, slips off pedestal onto cockpit floor; captain picks it up and only now sees reverse side which is impeccably printed:

'Dalton's Compleat Thirde Pilote—guide to Apollo 109 fuel conservations in the Mach .84 mode, with all four burning—after burn shut off.'

1855 Hours

Cabin supervisor takes crew order for meals. Captain and co-pilot order different food to guard against possible stomach upsets.

The captain told the co-pilot that when they returned on the weekend, he was going down to Leenane for a week's sea fishing in Killary.

Uncle Frank told me that when he was nineteen years old, he sat on an upturned porter barrel in a pub beside Killary, and drank pints with a sailor of the mighty British Atlantic fleet. The battleship was anchored a few hundred yards away in the inlet, because Killary is one of the finest deep water anchorages in Western Europe.

1956 Hours

Position 50 West. In touch with Gander on Very High Frequency.

'Gander clears the Shamrock 109 to the Kennedy airport on North American Route 57; Flight Level 350 not available—climb to and maintain 330, squawk A2100 on transponder and ident.'

The frequency was set up on the transponder and the little black button pressed. This momentarily duplicated the strobe on the Canadian radar screen and positively identified Shamrock 109.

2017 Hours

Flight conditions very smooth at 33,000 feet. Engine fuel consumption was now 10¼ tonnes per hour.

2025 Hours

Captain had his meal. The food was tastefully arranged on a small tray, which he had placed on his lap. He had pushed his seat back from the controls.

Cabin supervisor took the technical log and sat in the spare cockpit seat. She wrote in her snags, and as she went along she discussed them with the third pilot; when they had finished with the snags he sipped one of the cups of coffee which she had brought into the cockpit, and he spoke to her about her recent holiday in the Caribbean. . .

The Blue Danube sounded delightful as the music swelled and ebbed and paused, and then rushed on passionately just as Strauss had intended; every instrument gave of its sound in turn when the rest of the orchestra faded, and then the individuality of the violin, piano or cello and the brass became predominant. The melody hung magically in the tropical air, and only the officers of the regiment and the rustle of the dancers were missing.

The waltz tempo increased to its climax, and quite abruptly, but in complete harmony, with no lazy notes or late finishers, the music stopped. There was no regiment, nor would there ever be one; there was no conductor either, and no sheet music to bedeck dimly lit stands: we were 4000 miles from Vienna, the musicians were negroes, and all the instruments were steel drums.

This unusual method of making music originated in Trinidad during World War II. There the military had discarded the many drums in which they had stored their fuel and oil supplies; the enterprising locals made them into musical drums—steel drums—hence the name—steel band.

2027 Hours

'Gander Control now clears Shamrock 109 to climb to and maintain Flight Level 3500. Cleared Inertial Navigation System direct to Kennebunk; in ten minutes change to Moncton Control.'

Crew inserted the direct route to Kennebunk in the navi-

29

gation computers.

Co-pilot disengaged the height lock and dialled in 35,000 feet on the altitude select, and at the same time he moved the pitch control to start the aeroplane in the climb; the third pilot had leaned forward to adjust the throttles to give climb power.

2045 Hours

Captain finished his meal of chicken; co-pilot now has his steak. Third pilot places his food tray on the shelf in front of the instrument panel.

The sun, which had beamed through the cockpit windows with such unrelenting brilliance, sank down into a crimson bed of clouds, and shrouded the contrail of Lufthansa up ahead with a fiery glow.

The four trails of chilled white condensation had poured out from the engines as separate streams to some distance behind the aeroplane, where now they combined to form two; a half a mile further back it was one, and all the time the setting sun daubed the twirled rings of the jet efflux with darkening red.

2054 Hours

A flickering anti-collision light just overhead was now all that was luminous of Lufthansa 467.

*   *   *

The Irish jumbo flew on into the west; down over Kennebunk and into the New York control area. . .

2213 Hours

'Shamrock 109 descend to Flight Level 200 (20,000 feet), squawk A1500. . .

The air traffic controller's voice came through the muted loudspeakers: 'Shamrock 109, I have a target: he is in your nine o'clock position and passing one thousand feet below.'

'Positive contact,' replied the captain—'I have the DC 10 in sight. . .'

Uncle Frank senior was an authority on aircraft identification during World War II; his descriptions may have been colloquial, but at the same time they were strikingly accurate in depicting what he actually saw. Many a JU 88 nosing its way around the Irish coast was correctly spotted by Uncle Frank as a 'Single wing German bummer', and our antiquated biplanes were dubbed by him with equal authority as 'Wan engined double wingers'.

What Uncle Frank did not know, and neither did the Irish authorities until late in the war, that German reconnaisance planes, and their submarines, laid a number of weather reporting stations in the waters around the Irish coast.

The apparatus resembled a torpedo in size and shape, and they floated vertically in permanent positions and lay low in the sea; at set hours a mechanism opened the top of the cylinder and extended sensing probes: a radio transmitter then relayed the local temperature, pressure, humidity, wind direction and speed. When the observations were completed the probes retracted, the cover closed and the stations hugged the surface of the water, unseen by the Irish coast watchers. Their presence was only detected when one broke from its moorings and was washed up on the coast.

Uncle Frank never knew what a radio sounding balloon was, but like many other country people at the time, he saw them and correctly deduced that they were 'some new fangled yoke connected with the war.'

Both the Allies and the Germans used these devices extensively for sampling distant weather conditions: when released they drifted with the wind and relayed information similar to their counterparts in the sea. Eventually the radio ballon ascended to such a height that it burst in the upper atmosphere, but not before it had transmitted a considerable amount of valuable information from normally

31

inaccessible skies.

Were Uncle Frank alive today, his comments would be equally colourful, and then his outstretched palm would strike you on the chest and he'd say: 'Never mind about all those new fangled yokes, wait until I tell you what happened the German commercial traveller and the donkey on the road to Kenmare. . .

2230 Hours

'Shamrock 109—change to New York Approach' — they were now being manoevred by radar for landing.

2235 Hours

Captain ordered: 'Descent Approach Check.'

Crew progressed through the listed items.

Captain called: 'Flaps One.' Co-pilot made the required selection, but after 30 seconds both he and the third pilot said: 'No joy Skipper; something's wrong.'

Captain replied: 'Go ahead with the alternate system.'

Third pilot opened the ABNORMAL AND EMERGENCY checklist and went down through the details with the other pilot. He glanced at the captain and said: 'OK Skipper—stop worrying about it; you just fly away and leave the problem to us.'

2237 Hours

'Shamrock 109—what's your speed. I told you to slow down to 180 knots.'

'Sorry New York—we have a problem with the flaps.'

'OK Shamrock—do you want emergency equipment standing by?'

'Negative New York—we will be able to commence normal approach in five minutes.'

'OK Shamrock 109. I'll vector you out of the traffic pattern; turn right to a heading of 340 degrees. . .'

Ten minutes later the big jet was safely on the ground. It was 5.47pm local time. . .

*   *   *

At eight o'clock New York time, the crew were at their hotel in Manhattan. Two hours later some were in bed, and others were having a light snack in the coffee shop; two girls had gone uptown for a meal with the co-pilot, and the captain was across the street having a beer with the third pilot. By his wrist watch it was three in the morning; the clock over the bar counter was reading 10pm.

From arrival to departure on the following night, they would spend 26 hours in a different time zone and this was now their common factor, and they would each experience to varying degrees, the effect of a change on their circadian rhythms. Having been exposed to a five hour time displacement during this short overnight stay, they would fly back the next night into the dawn of their own natural time environment, and also into another five hour change with its consequent effects.

The term circadian can be broadly taken to mean a span of twenty-four hours; it is an ideal period for scientists to study man's reactions, because the major rhythms in human behaviour are closely allied to the physical cycles of day and night. In the Arctic, where seasonal changes bring long hours of daylight or alternatively many hours of darkness, the Eskimo does not evidence the usual circadian rhythms, although his social pattern reflects it to some degree.

Every creature that lives in our world possesses a rhythm of its own, which it acquired by its existence in a particular climatic environment, and its exposure to set patterns of light and darkness, sunrise and sunset.

There are the obvious cycles of gastric functions and the discharge of body wastes, sleep periods and the usual rhythms of temperature, heart beat and blood pressure. There would seem to be a twenty-four hour variation in the state of the nervous system, which determines the degree of mental fatigability at various hours of the day; the highest body temperature, best performance rate and lowest fatigability are

33

all reached, almost simultaneously, in the afternoon.

Inevitably then, there is a reaction when these rhythms are removed from their source of origin; the reaction varies with the individual, but most aircrew who experience time zone transition have developed a flattened or more stable form of circadian rhythm—in other words they get used to it.

A stopover time of 26 hours in North America is normally regarded as the minimum turn around period for crews who operate to there from Ireland, and its byproduct is a half exposure to a time zone change, with in consequence a limited reaction to its effects. On return it usually requires three nights until the sleep pattern reverts to normal; the problem being that the metabolic clock is still partially on American time. But now back to our crew at the hotel. . .

They are on a 26 hour stopover, and after retiring between 10 and 1am many would obtain 7 hours sleep: all generally awaken at 5, and then with some unable to return to slumber again. They will usually get up at 9 that morning, and then vary considerably in the quantity and content of their food intake during the day.

Prior to pick up that evening, most of them would endeavour to rest for a few hours, but sleep would not be possible for all.

After the homeward journey for this Irish crew, an almost standard sleep formula emerges: an initial period of 4 to 5 hours the morning of return, followed by perhaps up to 10 hours that night. Some difficulty might be experienced the next night in obtaining their usual quota of sleep, but the rest rhythm would be normal by the third day.

The rostering regulations permitted the male crew to fly out again after two days off—that would be three nights at home, but the next two tours of duty had to be separated by not less than three days, then the pattern repeated itself. The rules differed slightly for the air hostesses—they were scheduled for three days rest after each Atlantic trip.

Scientific studies of the sleep pattern associated with this type of time zone change reveal a sleep shift rather than a sleep loss; in other words, over the period in question the total number of hours of sleep obtained would equate that of a normal person not displaced from their usual time region, although the portion of the day or night during which it was obtained would differ greatly. A sleep deficit for aircrew would be linked to longer and more frequent trips involving time zone changes, and this could be characterised by the added problem of disturbed sleep.

The factors considered in the preparation of flight crew rosters are based on the fundamentals which have been considered but research on the subject is far from complete. Perhaps the answer would be to have an all Eskimo crew, but even they would have to be domiciled back at the pole before they acquired the rhythms of their warmer brethren!

I was still in a reflective mood when I reached my hotel bedroom; I sat in an easy chair and had a few quiet drinks, and I filled that room with ghosts of many departed friends. I wondered what the two Uncle Franks would have said about the time change problem: one, I know for sure, would have wanted to talk about it over several pints of stout, but the other would almost certainly slap me on the chest with his broad outstretched palm and say: 'They'll never believe that in Killala.'

CHAPTER THREE

PASSENGERS

Wing thy way through azure sky,
Sing thy heart in pleasures nigh.
Ring thy praise for all who fly.

The giant Boeing had crossed the ocean and was descending towards the coast; the pilot had already announced that they would be making their landfall over north Mayo, and then turning south to Shannon.

Hans Palfz, one of the passengers, was a German by birth, but he was an Irish citizen since 1946. He was seated beside a cabin window, and he looked down with renewed interest in the hope of seeing the soft lush green foothills of Nephin. The plane flew in over Killala, and then near Lough Conn and Castlebar; over to his right Clew Bay was shimmering in the morning sunlight with the glass surface of its waters indented by islands of every shape and size. The blue haze tinted mountains of Connemara edged down to Galway Bay, and the Aran Islands lay in the western sea like long wet sods of turf.

He remembered when he had parachuted out of those very skies from a Heinkel bomber. His thoughts drifted back across the years, and the lazy drone of the jumbo's throttled motors lay gentle on his memory in contrast to the harsh sound of the Heinkel's Jumos, deliberately desynchronised to confuse the listening device of the anti-aircraft batteries. . .

The Heinkel 111 came in over the Wexford coast at 12,000 feet, and Hans Palfz in the auxiliary cockpit seat peered at the green glow of the clock on the instrument panel, and estimated that he would be dropped at 0145 hours. The year was 1941.

The navigator's voice came over the intercom: 'Herr Leutnant—I now make it 59 minutes to the position.'

The bomber droned on through neutral skies. . .

'Better get your things together Hans,' the pilot said— 'Auf Wiedersehen my friend, and do not jump until the bloody red light comes on.'

Hans left the cockpit and clambered back through the cabin; a crewman helped him on with his parachute and equipment pack. He clipped the ripcord to the hook beside the door, and when the red light flashed he jumped through the opening into the darkness.

He felt the parachute jerk out above him and arrest his fall, and now he floated down through the night listening intently to the friendly but fading beat of the Heinkel's engines, as the bomber returned to Germany.

The drone of the plane had disappeared, but Hans was still descending through cloud, where dense water droplets streamed over his face and goggles and soaked through the heavy leather clothing. He removed one hand from the shroud lines of the parachute and brought his wrist down in front of his face; the luminous dial of the tiny altimeter read 1,500 metres—he should soon be out of the cloud now he thought, that was of course if the Luftwaffe meteorologist was correct in his forecast.

At 1,000 he was praying, because the mountain was 810 at the peak and then, exactly at 500 metres he came out of the stratus, and the isolated lights of farmhouses, and the more vague clusters of small towns came into view. The lights were so dispersed that they confirmed for him what he already knew—the sparseness of the population; then again, he thought, it was early in the morning and there was probably at least a partial blackout.

He was desperately trying to find his bearings, comparing what he saw with what was indelibly impressed upon his mind—a Luftwaffe night photograph of the area. He held his wrist level and identified south on the compass; he pulled himself round by the shroud lines until he was facing that direction. Yes, he was now certain where he was —about 15 kilometres north of Castlebar, but he appeared to be too far to the west; he dragged down one side of the canopy to spill its lift and drifted slowly eastwards; at 300 metres he peered anxiously at the ground for the indentification signal—yes, there it was, the rays of the Irish agent's flashlight signalling a succession of Morse code V's.

He manoeuvred the canopy towards the signal and prepared for the landing, but the ground came up faster than expected and his feet crashed through the leafless branches of a chestnut tree. The twigs bit at his clothing and then at his face, until the silken parachute became ensnared in the branches and broke his fall, but he stumbled into a thicket of blackberry briars; the thorns pierced his heavy trousers and clawed at his hands and face—'Gott in Himmel', but Division 2, German intelligence, at Frankfurt, had done its job well, when the swear came from his mouth it was in English. . .

Palfz and the Irish agent assembled the transmitter in the attic of the farmhouse. No light escaped—they checked that carefully; the place was cold and draughty, but it served its purpose, and he sat there night after night and tapped out his messages to Division 2 at Frankfurt.

Despite the enthusiasm of his Irish friend, Hans rapidly came to the conclusion that the information they were sending was valueless, and that the intelligence section at Frankfurt was becoming confused with his contacts. He brooded on his failure, and became disillusioned with his mission when he realised its futility. He longed to be back with his comrades as an ordinary solider—he knew his old regiment was still in Norway and he wondered what had become of his pals; he knew too that the RAF was bombing the Reich heavily, and he feared for the safety of his father and mother.

Something far more subtle was sapping away his dedication, and that something was the charm of one of the local girls. She was a trainee nurse in Dublin, but she came home frequently on weekends and they had many happy hours together. She may have had her suspicions as to what he was, but never voiced them.

How often had he watched the old steam engine Ben Bulben, whistling and puffing and coming in with the Dublin train; the light from the engine cab and the carriages running faintly along the moist bogland near the track and mirroring dimly in the bog pools, until the train chugged along near the goods sheds and the water tower and into the station. Grinding brakes, escaping steam, opening carriage doors, and the guard got his baton for the next section of the line. Suddenly it was all over for another couple of weeks—she had gone back to the city.

It was the simple things that he remembered most in her absence: the damp clinging fog that often lay on the hedges by the road to the railway station, and the way in which it traced the labours of the spiders with tiny globules into glistening silver threads.

He was haunted by the wild cry of the blackbird when it had rushed from its nest to seek sanctuary in a high tree, startled by the tumbling can of blackberries as he took her in his arms for the first time. The sweet scent of the hay tantalised his nostrils, because in the twilight of that lazy summer he lay there many times with his arms around her.

His work continued until early 1942, when the soft voice of the local Garda sergeant put an end to his clandestine existence. He heard the policeman's voice through the closed trapdoor: 'Come down sonny—quietly, and they'll be no shootin'. I have a few army lads here with me.' . . .

Germany surrendered in August 1945, and Hans Palfz was released from prison; he made his way to the German legation. In the building the staff were packing bulky files and office equipment, and there was a distinct smell of burning paper—he hustled past and down the long dark corridor that led to the office of the official who had visited him in jail.

'You will return to Germany of course, to the Fatherland who needs us all in this sad moment of defeat. . .' the voice droned along in the monologue that was strangely familiar to him in its emphasis on words like 'orders' and 'must'. He gave his answer by banging the door of the office with such force that the picture of the Fuhrer crashed down to the floor.

He caught the evening train from Westland Row to Ballina, and long after they had pulled out of Dublin, the web of splinters in the glass of that photograph still inched across the surface, until the face of the leader was totally obscured and all was silent in the deserted room. . .

Jumbo did not make a smooth landing at Shannon, and the jolt brought Hans back to reality. When they reached the terminal he made his way up to the forward exit. There was a pilot standing at the door, and the memories seared across his brain again—he thought of Schultz, the navigator of the Heinkel, and he almost said aloud: 'You'll never be dead to me Schultz as long as that young man is alive.'

* * *

Monsignor Patrick James O'Neill was born of Irish parents in Milwaukee. He had a rough childhood because his home was in the gut of that city, and he had fought innumerable street battles with German and Italian gangs; but the only mark that these experiences left with him was a deep enduring feeling for the plight of the poor and the underprivileged.

From the first day that he had been an altar boy in All Saints, the priesthood held a compelling fascination for him. In the beginning, it was the rich silks and the exotic designs of the vestments combined with the faint red glow of the sanctuary lamp and the lingering perfume of the incense: these things stimulated his imagination and led him into a

40

daily fantasy of mystery, with priests intoning strange and important sounding texts in Latin. Best of all, he was a part of the impressive ceremonies, and he gave the responses clearly although he never understood one word of what he was saying. His red soutane and white surplice gave him a position of importance that he would never have attained with the gang.

As he grew older he began to understand what it was really all about, and the fascination of a child deepened into a vocation which he locked in his heart until the day he finished school. His parents could not afford the seminary fees, and he worked as a labourer on the railroad until he had saved enough money to pay for himself. That was why, when he was ordained in 1956, he was thirty-five years of age. . .

Now it was the summer of 1973, and the monsignor was going to Ireland for the first time; his father had a brother in Sligo and he would motor up there from Shannon. He slipped into the men's room at Chicago airport and changed from clerical garb into a light suit.

He had been alotted seat 39B on the jumbo; he was the only occupant of the row of three, which was directly in line with the galley serving that part of the aeroplane. Deirdre Keogh was one of the girls working that galley.

Deirdre was twenty-three, tall and very goodlooking; she had a beautiful head of auburn hair and a thirty-six inch bust to go with it—and she knew it. Rarely have I seen a figure to compare with hers when she wore that white bikini on the beach at Boston.

The lights were turned down in the cabin, and Deirdre together with two other hostesses were looking after the last of the tired children: one was a small infant being fed from a bottle whilst its mother snatched a few hours rest.

'Sit down here Miss—take the weight off your feet for a minute,' said Paddy O'Neill, as he offered her a cigarette.

'Thank you but I am not allowed to smoke in front of the passengers.'

41

'Never mind, if somebody is looking, I'll pretend it's mine.'

She handed the baby to one of the other girls, took a cigarette and sat down beside him. They chatted for about twenty minutes, mostly about Deirdre until she asked: 'What business are you in?'

'I'm a priest,' he replied.

'Oh, I didn't realise that, Father,' she rose to go.

'What difference does that make, Deirdre. Bring me another Irish, and we'll finish our chat.'

She brought the whiskey, and as she handed him the glass he said: 'You are a very pretty girl.' She thought, 'Oh God, not one of those.' He sensed her slight disdain and hastened to open the little black letter case which he always carried. He took out a photograph and gave it to her saying: 'That's me over on the right, beside the two little boys.'

'Where was it taken, Father?'

'In a leper colony in Brazil where I work. They are charming people, but they have never seen such a lovely face as yours. There's a shortage of beauty there, Deirdre, and a shortage of nursing sisters; maybe you would be interested? . . .

At the edge of a rain forest in Brazil there is a small missionary hospital serving a leper colony, and a tall very good looking sister with auburn hair works there. I would recognise that figure anywhere: I admired it first on the beach at Boston.

* * *

Phelim Toner owned a bar in the Bronx. He was forty now and coming back to Ireland to marry a Cavan girl, and take her back with him to the States. His flight out of Kennedy was delayed, and he went up to the cocktail lounge for a drink. He sat at the only vacant stool at the counter and ordered a double scotch on the rocks.

The man beside him turned around; he was a small man

42

with ginger hair and a freckled face, and a little tweed hat perched jauntily on the back of his head. A green boarding card was tucked into his breast pocket.

'I knew it,' he said, 'I just flaming well knew it. It's yourself Phelim and you not a day older since we were with Johnston in the National School.'

'Mick Cooney, Mick Cooney,' said Phelim, and with each repetition of his name he pumped his hand all the harder. They were well oiled when the flight was called. . .

'Captain, there's two fellows in row 37 well jarred, and making a terrible nuisance of themselves.'

'Don't give them any more drink, Mary.'

'We stopped serving them, but I'm afraid they have their own flasks, or they may have got at the duty free.'

'I'll go down and have a word with them.' . . .

Two hours later Phelim locked himself in one of the toilets and couldn't get out. It was just as well because he threw up into every niche of that little room; he fell asleep on the lavatory. Meanwhile Cooney had managed with an air sick bag. Phelim was liberated when a hostess discovered that the wash room was engaged for an unusual length of time. She then hastily relocked the door, and stuck an 'out of order' sign on it.

They were almost sober by the time they had landed at Shannon, but the captain off loaded them; his cabin crew had taken all the abuse they could stand.

When Mick Cooney left the plane he insisted on taking the air sick bag with him; he knew what he was doing; his false teeth were in there—somewhere.

*   *   *

Mr Baily made a social call to the shop of his friend Abdul. The jeweller motioned towards the beaded curtains behind the counter and Baily followed him and sat down at the desk in the corner of the small office. The place was warm and the strong sunlight of the Lebanon streaming through its stained glass window threw strange coloured shadows over the bric-à-brac in the room.

Abdul handed him a piece of curved metal approximating to half the size of a cigarette case.

'That is gold Meester Baily—pure gold. Twenty more times for value in India than here in Beirut. I ask the favour that you would bring some to India for me. There will be a gift of £500 for you, and no risk with the Indian customs peoples. You see, I make the gold up in an especially nice leather belt that nobody takes notice. When you arrive at Bombay airport, a taxi drive will call your name and bring you to your hotel. You will see—no risk, you just leave the belt on the seat of the taxi when you get out.'

Baily was not convinced.

'Ah Jim—you look anxious; there is now £750 in it for you. Indian customs very nice peoples and not too strict. Customs only looking for alcohol—no risk I tell you. What you theenk?'

Baily was thinking all the time. He was an agent for an American engineering company, and he was flying to Bombay for a week of conferences. His returns in the last two years had been down on target, and the company was pressing him hard. £750 was an unexpected gift from the gods, and since he travelled to Bombay frequently, if he pulled this one off then he was sure to be asked to do it again; there was little risk, and it was only slightly illegal not like drugs and that sort of thing.

He was a lonely man; he was divorced and there had been no family. He had also exhausted the night life in Beirut, and this seemed a chance of a really exciting challenge, away from lousy champagne and the cheap perfume of Arab night club hostesses. . .

His fears now seemed like a bad dream, and he enjoyed his lunch in the jumbo as it flew high over Teheran. He followed the meal with a couple of expensive brandies, and whiled away the hours to Bombay leafing through the flimsy sheets of the special air edition of the London Times.

44

He paid scant attention to the passengers sitting beside him, but several times he placed his hands reassuringly on the belt and pressed it down firmly against his hips. The belt proved to be so comfortable that even this anxiety disappeared, and he settled fully to his Times.

Customs at Bombay's Juhu airport was a formality; like Abdul had said, they appeared to more concerned as to whether or not he was carrying liquor rather than anything else.

He picked up his bag and walked out confidently through the swing doors; a tall turbaned young man was chanting: Meester Baily—Meester Baily.'

He watched the throbbing crowds from the window of the cab as he had done countless times before. They passed the familiar bazaars, and the clamour and the smells he relished now because his mood was buoyant and he was flushed with the success of his first smuggling venture. He had beaten the system and would go on to do it again and again.

The heat in the taxi became oppressive and his braces began to stick to his shoulders; he placed his thumb under one side to ease it—every nerve of his body electrified in terror as he tore his hands down to where the belt should have been. He remembered clearly that he had been sitting in toilet 5L, when the pilot announced on the public address system that they would be landing at Juhu in ten minutes...

* * *

'Captain, there's a beautiful little girl in seat 21C. Would you ever come down and talk to her; she's an unaccompanied minor, and a perfect little pet.'

I replaced the cockpit telephone on its holder, undid the safety belt and pushed the seat back along its rails. As I put on my tunic and cap the co-pilot said: 'I saw her getting on at Philadelphia. Skipper, you'll be very taken with her.'

Sure enough, she was a beautiful child and she wore a

45

large label pinned to her dress which read:

'Are you going on holiday to Ireland, Kathleen?' I asked. 'No Captain,' she replied. 'My mammy and daddy were killed in an automobile accident, and I am going to live with my Uncle Joe.'

'How old are you, Kathleen?'

'Eleven, last fall.'

'Where are your brothers and sisters?'

'I don't have any, sir.'

'Are you enjoying the flight?'

'Gee it's just marvellous, and the stewardesses want me to pour out the orange juice for the passenger's breakfast.'

'Did you like our film?'

'I saw it before, on television' . . .

Joe Carbury was older than his brother Fiontan, from whom he had heard nothing since his departure to the States fifteen years before; that was until this particular morning, when the postman arrived at his door with an airmail letter from America. He unfolded the letter and laid it flat upon the table. He read it with his wife.

Dear Mr Carbury,

It is my unpleasant duty to inform you that your brother Fiontan Carbury, and his wife Jasmine Lily Carbury were both killed in an automobile accident in the city of Philadelphia.

In the event of Mrs J. L. Carbury's death, your brother's will had named you as ward of the child, Kathleen.

At our expense, Kathleen will be placed on an Irish Airlines 747 charter flight out of Philadelphia International Aug. 12 1973. Arrival Shannon is due 9 o'clock local time.

I presume you will be in a position to meet the child. Please cable confirmation upon receipt of this mail.

46

May I offer you our condolences, sir. Your brother and his wife were warm and sincere friends of my partner and I,

Yours faithfully,
Anselm J. Schwitz
Attorney-at-Law.

'Will you come to Shannon with me,' Joe asked his wife. 'No love, I'll stay and get the child's room ready. I want it to be real nice for her, the poor little mite. God rest Fiontan's soul and his young wife, but the little girl is a gift from heaven and we with none of our own.'

At two o'clock she heard the crunch of the gravel under the wheels of the car, and her heart pounded with excitement She rushed to the hall door, and Joe met her as he came in from the yard.

'Where is she, where is she?'

'Getting her little gifts out of the car; she has a present for you. She is an absolute beauty, the image of Fiontan, and not at all as rude as those kids of Sadie's. You'll love her, and I know that after a while she will fit in like a glove with the rest of the little girleens around here. She's coming now.'

His wife ran out to meet the child. She was black.

*   *   *

Boris Severyanych was a happy man. He was normally abstemious, but today, as he sat at a window table in the passenger lounge of Moscow's Sheremetievo airport he indulged in several vodkas with his caviar.

It was early spring, and the melting snow revealed an all embracing monotonous brown grey tint. Russia was covered with the robe of departing winter, and it swept and undulated from the Polish border to Moscow itself and over the Kremlin walls; here the onion domes of the czar's churches caught the rays of the watery sun in dull reflections. On the grey swept to the Urals and over the Vasugane swamp to the Sea of Okhotsk; but soon the giant would recover from its torpor, and all of Russia would come alive in blossom to herald a fruitful abundance.

Boris was thinking of these things, but yet his heart was not sad; for the first time in his sixty-five years of life, he would not be part of that spring. Boris Severyanych was happy, happy to leave his beloved Russia, and free at last to write about her, free to express his thoughts and feelings as an intellectual must do. He had received an exit permit—to leave Russia for ever.

His mood was elated as he recognised the aeroplanes of the western nations, and parked on position 14 was also the splendid Tupolev TU 134 with its two uprated Soloiev turbofan engines. He watched with added interest as the baggage truck trundled out to the Tupolev, and he knew that the large brown trunk was his, and within—his pulse had quickened—were the manuscripts of his books which the Soviets would not allow him to publish. Secretly and safely he had stowed them away in the false sides of the trunk; who could detect such a construction—the space between the sides was but 3 millimetres wide. He had laboriously transcribed the texts to the flimsiest of paper.

'Passengers now boarding for Aeroflot's Flight 335 to Vienna'—the public address system echoed through the departure lounge.

Now he looked out of a cabin window and watched the brown grey earth of Mother Russia disappear for ever as the Tupolev rotated and entered cloud.

At Vienna he had a three hour stopover before the departure of a Pan American 747 to New York, and there was a noisy little party of Russian emigrés in the Bolera bar.

'Pan American announces the departure of its Flight 101 from Vienna to Paris and New York. . .

Severyanych awoke to the sound of the thrust reversers, as the 747 decellerated on runway 22L at the Kennedy airport, New York.

Before he had arrived by the planemate at the terminal,

a Pan American traffic agent in the building was saying to his assistant: 'Hey Hank, better meet 101, there's a Russian guy called Severyanych on the flight. I have a telex from Aeroflot at Moscow to say that his baggage went by mistake on their flight 101 to Leningrad. They say that they will have to run a security check on it before forwarding. Just meet the guy Hank, it's not Pan Am's fault. . .

*　　*　　*

The waters of the ornamental lake had receded with the summer drought, and the surface was scum covered with soapy foam that oozed over exposed muddy stretches and edged against the bordering rocks. Beer cans and bottles, twigs and rags were jammed against the bars of the drainage trap; here the filthy waters finally escaped, and made their way down through the bowels of the city to seek purification in the sea.

The heat of the summer had torn the life from the green grass of New York's Central Park and exposed great patches of baked earth. Under the shelter of the trees, some of the flotsam of humanity slumbered in drugged and drunken stupor, whilst others of their calling scavenged from trash cans and threaded another hopeless day along the shaded walks.

Paddy O'Meara had also abandoned society for the god of drugs, the flop houses and the sleazy taverns. With the pavement or the park for his bed, he picked his cigarettes from the street and ate from the garbage can; he was 32, but what was left of his mortal coil was 70. He shuffled along the parkway: 'Spare a dime mister for a cup of coffee; spare a dime' . . .

Now he had collected the ten dollars that he needed for his fix, and he slouched on a bench to wait for the dope peddlar who came that way at midday. Young sparrows chirped about his feet and hopped around the metal hoops of the seat in search of crumbs; small fish ventured to the surface in the deeper parts of the lake, and a cool breeze puckered the dirty expanse and teased it into life.

His dulled senses became more conscious of his surroundings, and his mind wandered back to Galway and the sweet memories of his youth. He had come to the land of opportunity at the age of 27 to make his fortune, and send half of it back home to his widowed mother.

All that was left of his manhood and his promise was in the pocket of his greasy jacket: the torn remnants of an airline ticket.

CHAPTER FOUR

CITY IN THE SKY

Great metal thing
With eagle grace arise,
And in thy bulk
Contain humanity in its disguise.

The Boeing 747, which I am currently flying, is the largest commercial aeroplane ever built and was conceived in the 1960's. The design of the machine was based on intense market research, which concluded that a large aeroplane would be required for the predicted loads of the 1970s and 1980s. Due to a general world depression in every aspect of industry including aviation, and an unprecedented escalation in oil prices, the projected loads did not materialise; nevertheless the concept was correct and large aeroplanes, highly economical and profitable when fully laden, are here to stay.

To prove and test the integrity of the aircraft structure, and the ability of its many electrical, hydraulic, and mechanical systems to function capably in a wide variety of circumstances, an extensive and lengthy check programme was set up by the Boeing company. Five aeroplanes were tried out in the air for 1400 hours before the big jet was certified for commercial service in December 1969.

Two further aeroplanes were subjected to structural and fatigue probing on the ground; these would never fly, but were used by the Boeing engineers to prove the soundness of their construction. The fatigue evaluation programme subjected the grounded aeroplanes to stresses and strains for long periods. The experiments imposed loads on their structures which were far greater than would be experienced in flight; wings and tail and other critical parts were deliberately cracked or even sawn through, and exposed to further severe tests for the equivalent of 12,000 hours actual flying.

The 747 was the first wide body commercial aeroplane, and it possessed twice the passenger and cargo capacity of its predecessors. The main cabin is 20 feet wide and 185 feet long, and it is divided into five compartments; the pilot's cockpit is above the main deck, and behind it is a spacious lounge, reached by a circular stairway from the first class area beneath.

Although the navigation equipment is no bigger than an office drawer and as light as a typewriter, it can take that aeroplane automatically, and with uncanny accuracy to any place on earth. There are eighteen wheels to spread the weight of the monster on the ground, and thus each tyre exerts no more pressure than those of smaller jets.

Several large fuel tanks carry 39,000 gallons, and when the air supply system pressurises the cabin for comfortable flight, a ton of air is added to the weight of Jumbo.

It is difficult to imagine that when the Wright brothers made man's first-ever powered flight at Kitty Hawk, the distance flown was less than the length of the big Boeing.

The 747 typifies modern air travel in a pressurised cabin, flying at 560 mph at an altitude of 35,000 feet; it is a dramatic contrast with early days when one airline had to warn its passengers: 'The aircraft are closed, and travellers therefore do not need any special equipment. They should dress warmly however, especially in winter.'

*   *   *

Isaac Newton saw a little red apple fall from a tree, and from such a simple incident he is supposed to have evolved the laws of gravity and motion. One of these laws explains how a propeller, or a jet engine powers an aeroplane's flight: 'to every action, there is an equal and opposite reaction,' said Newton; both the propeller and the jet engine accelerate a mass of air to the rear of the plane and this generates a reaction which propels the machine forward. The greater the amount, and the speed of the propeller air, or of the gases escaping from a jet nozzle, the greater the thrust of that engine.

The piston driven propeller is limited in size and rotational speed, and therefore the thrust it produces is considerably less than that of a jet; the latter is able to develop much more power by giving greater acceleration to a smaller quantity of air.

The basic cycle, and the fundamentals of operation of a piston and a jet engine are the same. The jet takes in huge volumes of air and compresses it, fuel is added and ignited, and the subsequent expansion of the vapour drives the engine, and produces thrust as the mass of hot gases is expelled from the tail pipe. The propeller derives its energy from the power stroke of the pistons in the cylinders.

The motor car engine does exactly the same thing—it creates an expanding volume of gas whose energy is transferred, via a clutch, to a gear box to drive the wheels.

In simple practice the same principle is again evident in the water gathering buckets of the old mill wheels, and it must have been from such a mill that in 1791, an Englishman, John Barber, derived the idea of a gas turbine, because he patented a simple motor in that year. It was not until the 1930s that serious work started on an engine, and the experiments were independent of each other. Frank Whittle in England was not aware that Hans von Ohain in Germany was working on the same project: the construction of a practical aircraft jet engine.

The German's invention eventually powered the Heinkel 178, which was the first jet aeroplane to fly on 27 August 1939. Whittle's engine was installed in a Gloster G40 which gunned into the sky in May of 1941; both of these engines produced just 1,000 pounds of thrust, which is exactly the output of the auxiliary power unit in the tail of a Boeing jumbo, used to supply electrical and hydraulic power, as well as air conditioning, whilst the aircraft is on the ground.

The urgent military need at this time, for bigger and better conventional piston engines in increasing quantities, prevented the American firm of Pratt and Whitney from pursuing its own research with gas turbine aero engines. However, the war came to an end on the evening of 14 August 1945, and military production at their plants was brought to a standstill in a single day.

The factory continued to manufacture piston engines which powered many of the famous commercial and military aircraft of the immediate post war era. Although they were late starters with jet engines, massive research and development ultimately led to the production of such engines in enormous quantities—then came their largest unit, the JT 9D turbo fan giving 43,500 pounds of thrust. This is the powerplant fitted to the Boeing 747; it is eight feet in diameter at the inlet, twice the size of other engines, and yet is is smaller in length and emits very little smoke. The airflow through the motor is 1,500 pounds per second, and the large fan in the front, which is almost a propeller, produces three-quarters of the push.

The aero engines of today have been adapted to uses other than propelling aeroplanes, and there are a number employed in industry in Ireland. Such engines provide an instantaneous, economical and reliable source of enormous power from low grade fuels, such as diesel oil or natural gas; they are compact and clean, occupy little space, and do not require a large engineering staff to supervise them in operation.

For marine purposes, the gas turbine aero engine is gradually replacing the conventional steam turbine. Its fuel consumption is marginally higher, but this disadvantage is outweighed by many other considerations in its favour.

The engines are also ideal for pumping natural gas over

long distances from the gas fields of the world. The turbine uses some of the gas to power itself, and since the combustible is very clean there is little or no build up of unwanted deposits on its working parts; this factor contributes enormously to prolonging the life of the engine and maintaining its efficiency: one such power plant has given over 30,000 hours service, without attention.

It is more than likely then, that the deposits of natural gas and oil beneath the Celtic sea will be pumped ashore to refineries and consumers in Ireland by means of a gas turbine similar to the engines powering the Boeing jumbo jet. Remember then, when you are enjoying the fruits of those off-shore wells, that Frank Whittle and Hans von Ohain have contributed greatly to your pleasure, whether you are on land or sea or in the skies of Rosseau, Crosbie, FitzMaurice and Saul.

*   *   *

When our jumbo, *St Patrick*, rolled off the production line at the Boeing plant in Seattle, it took its place in the queue to have four of those splendid JT 9D's fitted. It was to be an interesting experience for the aeroplane, this mating with its engine companions; its body was primarily composed of aluminium alloys, and now it was consummating its purpose with titanium, nickel, cobalt and iron based super alloys.

The friction of the air flowing along its sleek shape in high speed could heat up its skin by as much as 35° C. but the engines could generate 846° C. without damage, and along those 65,000 parts which compose their structure, a wide range of operating temperatures would exist.

Each engine weighed 8,470 pounds, but how snugly those JT 9D's were attached to the wings in just a few hours, and how simply the aeroplane's pipes and electrical connections matched exactly with those of its powerful companions. The cowlings were placed in position, and as the last fastener was closed the big machine had acquired a feeling of poise and equilibrium, knowing that the centre of gravity was in the correct position, and that it would be able to trim itself to accommodate any type of load placed in the cabin or cargo holds; the powered tail unit could be adjusted from the cockpit to aerodynamically balance any weight distribution.

Now the jumbo was ready to fly, and what a splendid vehicle it would be to traverse the heavens and contain humanity in his disguise, with his goods and chattels tucked away in a voluminous belly. I know from flying that great metal thing that it must have a soul or an uncanny sensitivity, because it locks into the sky with an insatiable love for distance, and the further it flies the more it settles into the ethereal groove.

CHAPTER FIVE

SERVICE AND SUSTENANCE

O perfect creature of man's endeavour,
Perfection demands mechanical concord
And thy bowel replete with fuel and food.

Commercial aeroplanes require a twenty-four hour service from two important, but independent sources: maintenance and catering. One attends to the physical needs of the aeroplane and the other provides sustenance to its occupants.

The term 'maintenance' as applied to aviation, covers the day to day servicing of any flying machine; development of new projects, the study of returns and trends, and the quality control of all the work carried out on the plane is the responsibility of the engineering side of a maintenance organisation.

The total activity of this combination is then monitored by officials of the departments of civil aviation in the various countries; it is a feature of the system that the government authority licences an airline to carry out such work, and also permits it to supply similar services to foreign aircraft. The national flag carrier, Aer Lingus, has a worldwide reputation for the quality of its maintenance and overhaul, and each year large numbers of overseas operators place handsome contracts with the company for the servicing of their aeroplanes.

In the field of technical training, many nations have

chosen to send their young men to Ireland to learn the rudiments, and the finer points of aviation skills.

When an aeroplane such as a Boeing 747 is ordered by an airline from the manufacturer, provisioning for it would commence almost two and a half years before the anticipated date of delivery. The manufacturer's advice, combined with airline experience would indicate the number of spares required, and the frequency with which to reorder. The whole of the vast spares programme would then be banked in a computer, where the electronic brain would keep the tally and monitor the demand on stocks.

Every part of an aeroplane including the very spares themselves has a specified life of service stated in flying hours or total time. This span of time is always alotted by the manufacturers, who monitor the products in service and co-relate information received from airlines on any snags that may arise.

The delivery of an aircraft is followed by a continuous flow of service bulletins and recommendations, and worldwide operating experience of the type is shared amongst the operators.

*　　*　　*

The labour force of Aer Lingus would be typical in content to that of most airlines, with ten major trades predominant: mechanics, electricians, instrument technicians, radio engineers, sheet metal workers, carpenters, upholsterers, painters, cleaners and welders; in addition there are many other men whose jobs cover a variety of skills allied to such crafts. These experts carry out the daily inspections of the aeroplanes.

The big Boeings will have transit checks after each landing, with more comprehensive checks as the flying hours accumulate. By 1800 hours the inspection and routine work would be quite considerable, with much use of lubricants; there would be little wear and tear on the plane but the work would ensure that everything was in tip-top condition.

After flying for 12,000 hours the jumbos will be taken out of service and given a major overhaul. Now they will enter and remain in that hangar where lesser aeroplanes are almost completely dismantled in similar circumstances; but for them, Boeing's manufacturing techniques and sophisticated inspection methods allow their bulk to remain almost intact whilst engineers probe the surface and the innards with sonic and x-ray equipment.

No system that circulates fuel, oil, electricity, hydraulic fluid or water will escape the eagle eye of the inspector; during life on the line, there is a continuous programme of structural inspection that augments this routine. Finally, when they are resplendant in a new coat of livery, over 300 gallons of special preparations will have been sprayed from those paint guns.

When the aircraft is in passenger service, the provision of spares at the home base poses no difficulty, but in order to overcome the problem of supplying similiar support at out-stations the airlines have devised a pool system. By agreement, operators pool their spares at main airports, and each company, depending on its demands, contributes a set number of items to the common store. If an accessory is required by a plane, then the airline must replace the item in the pool within a reasonable time.

The Boeing jumbo is a popular machine with the mech-anics; it gives little trouble, and if it does the problem area is very accessible. The machine was designed in such a way as to have as many of its components as possible in the form of modules; this also eliminated the wasteful searching around to locate the snag. A fault could now be easily traced to a section of the aeroplane, and then the pack of fittings in that position removed and replaced by a fresh module. The defective part is subsequently examined and repaired at leisure in the workshop.

Occasionally the system slips, in a humourous but not serious way—I was browsing through a technical log recently and came across the following sequence of events:

The High Frequency radio had been snagged as unserviceable on three previous flights; ground rectification had restored power to the unit, but the set went dead on later flights.

Next, a third pilot, exasperated with the chain of events, wrote in the log: 'No. 2 HF now unserviceable for 4 flights. Please send it to Lourdes for a cure or change the set.'

Back at base the maintenance people decided to replace the radio and then made an entry in the log opposite the pilot's report: 'All Lourdes flights full. However, transmitter-receiver replaced and holy water sprinkled. System now checks out OK.'

All of the instrument readings, every gallon of fuel used, each pulse of a jumbo's engines are recorded at regular intervals in flight; they are later fed to a computer for analysis.

The speed, height, gravity forces, compass headings and many other parameters are traced continuously on the indestructible flight recorder. There is a voice recorder in the cockpit which tapes the pilot's conversations in the actual plane, or his transmissions to air traffic control.

It would seem then that the tranquility of your flight is preceded by a background of frantic mechanical activity but, as you now know, it is a well thought-out routine. The competent way in which your magnificent aeroplane makes its path across the skies of this planet in the hands of Irish pilots, is the direct result of expert and methodical work by equally competent Irish engineers.

*   *   *

Jet engines do not generally require the sophisticated fuels of their predecessors, whose exclusive thirst for the finest product of the refinery, high octane gasolene, made them expensive to operate. Kerosene is the fuel burned by a turbine engine, and domestic paraffin oil is essentially the same thing, only it has been improved by an additive which eliminates much of the carbon deposit and gives it a better flame. Nevertheless, there are many additional important quality requirements for aviation kerosene that make its manufacture and its handling a complex technical matter.

Aviation kerosene, as consumed by the massive Pratt and Whitney engines of the Boeing 747, must burn efficiently and cleanly and provide adequate energy for thrust. Many aeroplanes utilise the mass of fuel in their tanks as a cooling agent, and in the case of the jumbo the hydraulic fluid of its systems is cooled by passing it through heat exchangers suspended in the tanks. This has the added side effect of helping to heat the fuel itself, since outside air temperatures of minus 60°C. are not uncommon at the normal operating heights. However, this poses another problem, because the fuel which initially must resist chemical degradation in storage, must also do so when used as a heat transfer medium in an aircraft tank. Another primary requirement is that the kerosene must be incapable of chemically attacking the components of the complicated aircraft fuel system.

As with all petroleum products, aviation kerosene has to be free from dirt, rust, water and other contaminants, and it is interesting to realise that the fuel in the large storage tanks around the country is actually floating on a three foot depth of water. This arrangement ensures that the fuel does not come into contact with the base of the tank where the impurities gather; any residual water in the kerosene itself will gradually filter down to join the three foot layer at the bottom. Before the fuel is pumped into a plane's tanks, further tests are carried out to ensure that no water pollutes the kerosene.

The water base must be of acceptable quality, since there are organisms that will live and thrive in kerosene. Some years ago, the cause of a rash of fuel pump failures in an aircraft was traced to a foreign country of warmer clime. Here a parasite transferred to the fuel from the storage water, and perpetuated itself at an alarming growth rate in the bottom few inches of the aircraft's tanks. In a relatively short time it corroded the fuel pumps.

Lubricating oils circulating in a jet engine are exposed to very high temperatures, and therefore special synthetic lubricants have to be manufactured to cope with such conditions. These oils will not degrade under extremes and they keep the engine clean and do not evaporate in the low atmospheric pressure at high altitudes. Foaming was another difficulty with early engine oils, and special design features such as baffles were incorporated in the tanks to prevent it. The synthetic lubricant has an additive which almost eliminates the problem.

Kerosene for the engines of Irish aeroplanes comes mainly from the three million tons of crude oil that flows each year through the Whitegate refinery in Cork. That oil will have originated in the Middle East and Venezuela and, sent via the larger refinery at Milford Haven to Whitegate, from where it is delivered by tanker up the broad sweep of the Shannon river to the storage tanks at the airport.

The tanks from the ship run along the top of that very sea wall which, but a few years before, was part of a grand plan that never came to fruition: the wall encompassed the little artificial harbour, whose waters were to contain the anchorage for the transatlantic flying boats, feeding land based aeroplanes with passengers and freight for Europe.

From the depot tanks at Shannon, the kerosene flows to a hydrant system which enables planes there to be refuelled where they park, and thus dispenses with the older method of trucks. This arrangement of almost ship to aircraft hook-up is unique; the installation is even more unusual at London airport, because here aviation fuel is pumped directly from the refinery at Fawley to the storage tanks at Heathrow.

Large aeroplanes are fed with fuel from both sides at once, and the required amount is simply dialled in on the aircraft system. When the desired quantity is pumped on board the aircraft tanks signal the pressure hoses and the flow shuts off automatically. Unlike older aeroplanes the modern machine does not really have tanks as such, but utilises the internal structure of the wings to store its fuel.

The engines of the comparatively small fleet of Aer Lingus consume 55-60 million gallons of kerosene each year. Where then is it all going to come from as the demand increases—were enough of those single cell creatures buried in the bowels of the earth when our planet was young?

Recent discoveries of new oilfields have revealed a capacity that far exceeds the present day consumption. The wells in the North Sea near the Shetlands will eventually have an enormous production, whilst the ocean to the south-west of Ireland, the Celtic Sea, has promise of a further rich oil harvest. Undoubtedly in time the world resources of oil will be exhausted, but it is an impossible task to forecast the date. Meanwhile the development of different sources of energy to produce electricity, such as natural gas, atomic reactors and solar cells, will release a vast quantity of oil for other purposes.

The propulsive force for the flying machines of the future may not be derived from the carbon and hydrogen remnants of those slimy cells of long ago. Meanwhile, you are assured that the hundreds of millions of gallons of paraffin oil imbibed by those flying machines will be available in incredible quantities for many years to come.

From the airline point of view, the worry is not the availability of the fuel, but its cost. Although only about 10% of the distillation from the crude consists of aviation kerosene, the cost increase by the oil producing countries to the air companies is out of proportion, with a quadrupling of price during the past few years.

*　　　*　　　*

There is a saying that the shortest way to a man's heart is through his stomach, and since he takes that stomach into the air with him, it has to be fed but is the in-flight catering business overdone by the airlines?

Early efforts in air passenger catering ranged from snack lunches in cardboard boxes, to four course meals dispensed by stern looking stewards to languid travellers in airborne wicker chairs. 'Languid' is the appropriate word, since they must have felt awful flopping up and down for hours in those low and slow flying cumbersome biplanes. Light snacks became a necessity in the relatively faster monoplanes like the DC3, and now on long journeys, it is expected that a substantial amount of food and drink is available in the airborne larder. Considerable expense and wastage is involved in the provision of such meals, and it may well be that these amenities could be drastically reduced, with the saving passed on to the passenger.

The entrance to the flight kitchen complex at the Dublin airport is dominated by a weighbridge and an accounting officer; these facilities are necessary for all such organisations, to control the flow of provisions and equipment to the large storerooms in the building. The orderly design of the structure would suggest that it is a vast spares depot, and it is therefore difficult to realise that this is the larder, the preparation centre, the bar and catering supply, from which the jumbos and their many companions are serviced with food and drink, together with attendant condiments, cutlery, crockery, glassware and utensils.

Here is a bakery, a butchery, a cold room; here are food conveyor belts, chefs, mini chefs and white clad women; here are prawns and lobsters, cutlets, cauliflowers and cucumbers, potatoes and tomatoes. Here echoes the clank of a timeless chain belt that transports used utensils through an outsize washing machine.

The modern aeroplane has an immense appetite for prepared foods, and the daily output of this catering unit during the busy months of summer, totals five thousand main meals on trays, together with a huge number of light snacks. The dish in which the salads are served, measures about four inches; this means that if the total production for the months of April to September were placed end to end on the ground they would stretch for 180 miles, not to mention the millions of eggs, tons of meat and butter, thousands of gallons of milk, and all that stout, beer, whiskey, brandy and wine.

These enormous demands are met by daily deliveries of fresh Irish produce. The quality of the products is monitored closely and the variation in the menus is tailored closely to the taste of the passenger; there is a continual return of comment through the air hostess flight reports.

The technique of preparing such dishes differs considerably from hotel methods. Flight kitchens must pre-tray each meal as a complete unit, and usually the food has to be partially pre-cooked, since it is not possible to fully cook such a large number of meals in the aircraft ovens.

Inevitably there is waste in aviation catering; no matter how carefully the amounts are calculated, there is always something left over. The sick or reject factor with the passenger is impossible to assess accurately, and on the other hand since the customers have come to expect high class catering from the airlines, there must not be a shortfall in quantity either.

This then leads to the next problem, that of waste disposal. International health regulations prohibit the use of such foods for human or animal consumption, even though the waste may be in the form of intact sealed meals—thus the leftovers must be destroyed.

Now that you have some idea of the activity of the commissariat, let us visit there whilst the staff are loading the goodies for our fully booked jumbo, due to fly to North America. The capacity load will be: 24 first class, and 369 tourist passengers plus 19 crew members—a total of 412 meals with all the additives. Ignoring mundane things like tea, coffee, sugar and milk, the inventory contains such diverse items as 16 pounds of boiled sweets, 1,600 plastic glasses, 300 cocktail napkins, 10 gallons of orange juice, tooth picks and swizzle sticks, playing cards, newspapers and magazines, toilet sheets and paper towels by the thousand, razors and toothbrushes, slippers and eye shades, and most important of all: steaks and chickens, lobsters and prawns and salmon, salads and sauces, and enough spirits, beers and soft drinks to keep that City In The Sky going for several hours.

Bon appetit.

CHAPTER SIX

AIRPORT

Aeroplane, activity, arrival and car.
Cargo, corridor, customs and bar.
Departures, delays, despair and announcement.
Escalator, elevator, embarkation, excitement.

Napoleon declared that every French soldier carried a field marshal's baton in his knapsack; that pronouncement is valid today although not quite in the exact context that the emperor intended. It can be stated with equal certainty that every airline pilot has a route manual in his brief case. Unlike Napoleon's soldiers, he will not share that metaphorical change of promotion just because he carries one, but more dramatically, he guards the safety of his passengers because of the wealth of information given in that book.

In the map section will be found charts of the highways of the air as they exist over the earth's surface. Radio beacons, important positions, international air traffic control boundaries, ground height, principal bearings from radio stations: it is all there, and presented in such a way as not to confuse the pilot or bewilder the uninitiated. The weather broadcasting services of the aviation world are fully described together with an explanation of the code in which they broadcast their messages. In the radio coverage, almost everything that emits a bleep on earth and that may be used by aeroplanes is categorised.

You may rest assured that no matter what remote airfield on this globe that your transport is approaching, your pilots, some considerable time in advance will have reached down into their Napoleonic bag and taken out the airfield plate of Wirrabongo, Timbucktoo or wherever you may be. They will study the approach procedure, and organise their radio frequencies and settings accordingly; they will note the hazardous areas to avoid, and take special care to adjust their altimeters to the local barometric pressure so that the height read out is absolutely accurate. The page is kept conveniently to hand in the event that further information is required. You can see now that Napoleon might have had more in mind than a baton when he spoke about that knapsack.

The name of the airport is spelt very clearly at the top of each airfield page and the letters are large and unambiguous: there will be no mistake here. A small profile printed on the plate depicts the path of the aeroplane as it follows the approach procedures from the radio beacons to the runways. The lowest height to which an approach may be made is clearly specified, and also a fly away path in the event that weather conditions are too poor for a landing. The reverse side of the sheet details the runway lengths and the approach lighting systems.

All of these descriptions add up to one magical word— AIRPORT. This is the setting where romantic meetings take place, or lovers part in tears; here, husbands and wives may have to separate because of economic necessity; happy travellers revel, children frolic and commuters are brusque. Painters, peasants, poets and politicians, civil servants, clerics, dentists and doctors, engineers, entrepreneurs and everyman wait at sometime or other in the sunlight or the shadows of that airport.

Two hundred major airports dot the international scene. There are also many thousands of smaller airfields, private flying clubs, factory owned runways, together with the primitive grass strips and sand or earthen patches that serve the material medical and spiritual needs of countless small communities.

I remember a colleague, a missionary pilot priest, who went to aid a primitive community in Borneo. An ex-service pilot, a New Zealander, he had flown with Aer Lingus for a number of years, and saved most of his salary to pay subsequently for his education at an ecclesiastical college in Rome.

A special dinner was given to him by a group of his pilot and hostess friends, at which he was presented with an elaborately embroidered Celtic vestment. During the ceremony a voice from the back of the dining room interrupted and said: 'Larry, you know when you raise your arms to pray with that yoke on, the congregation reads "Fly Aer Lingus".'

This fine pilot priest was killed in a flying accident in the bush in Borneo, just a short time after he had arrived there. But to return to our airports. . .

A vast communication web entwines them, and distributes data on weather, runway conditions, radio aid serviceability, passenger loads and freight weights, aircraft schedules, road, rail and sea time-tables, onwards bookings, departure and arrival times, catering requirements, fuel loads and aircraft mechanical condition. The network utilises radio, telephone and teleprinter services to distribute the messages; closed circuit television relays information within the individual airports.

A handling agent, perhaps in Baltimore, can electronically interrogate a computer in Europe, and derive from its stored knowledge the names of the actual passengers booked on a particular flight. The detail is conveyed to him on the equivalent of a small television screen, and its transmission is instantaneous.

We likened before the contact and communication between individual aeroplanes to that of the members of a huge herd constantly harnessed to each other; how wonderful it is then that the hands of Marconi and Baird have reached out and touched almost every human being on earth, placing them in audio and visual communion whether on land, sea or in the air. Thanks to their inventions, man can view the distant wonders of our universe and listen to radio messages transmitted from unmanned space ships hurtling towards eternity.

The networks providing an airport with so many channels of contact are but one of the services and facilities that are available to the public, the airlines and the oil companies. Long distance communication usually requires the use of a cable to guarantee permanent and good quality contact, but more and more transmissions are being made through communication satellites which relay signals to earth, or to each other to extend the range. This capability is fitted to the 747 and will be used when regular satellite channels are established for civil aircraft.

Each international, or large domestic airport has within it all the services and technical refinements that would be found in a major town or city; the airport manager however, exercises authority over a far wider range of responsibilities than his municipal equivalent. At Shannon, for instance, there is even a special amphibious vehicle for search and rescue operations on the estuary; the unusual design enables it to operate on the mud flats in the vicinity. Mechanical units must also be available to handle snow and ice on the runway surfaces; constant patrols are required to keep flocks of birds away from the path of the aeroplanes as they taxi or take off, and new methods have to be continually devised to provide efficient bird scaring.

Some time ago I saw a large crow sitting on top of a bird scarer; every time the gun went 'bang' the bird flopped up in the air and then sat down on the barrel again—he was just going nowhere. Birds are a problem at airports: they tend to congregate on the concrete to keep their feet dry.

There are three main international airports in the Republic of Ireland: Shannon, Dublin and Cork. There are also many smaller aerodromes and landing strips throughout the country, and each one of them is licensed and inspected regularly by the state. In a different context, it is interesting to know that Shannon airport was 'licensed' in 1947 by the Customs Free Airport Act, and thus became the first duty free airport in the world; it still retains its pre-eminence as the largest and the best. A staff of 1,740 is currently employed by the state to run the three airports, and for example at Dublin airport alone, airline and related employment personnel further swell its population to 5,000.

The airfields and their maintenance, meteorological, radio and control services, the very airway corridors themselves are services provided by the state, and some of the expense involved is recouped at the airports by concession charges, and by rentals to airlines and other commercial companies. The largest amount of revenue accrues from landing and passenger load fees: landing charges are based on the weight of a fully laden aircraft, and a per-capita levy is also made for each embarking passenger. The landing charge for a Boeing 747 at an Irish airport is in excess of £500; these rates vary from country to country.

During the year 1973-1974, the total of flight movements at Irish airports came to 110,000. Aer Lingus, British Airways, Cambrian, Northeast, British Island, British Midland, Scandinavian, Iberia of Spain, Lufthansa the German carrier, Alitalia and KLM, Air Canada, Pan American, TWA and Seaboard World were the major airlines using our airfields. There were also French aeroplanes, Cubans, Yugoslavs, Poles, Bulgarians and Russians and many more casual visitors ranging from private and charter aircraft to military aviation of Irish and foreign origin.

The aircraft types were typical of any international scene, with every kind of Boeing, all the Douglas variants, Viscounts, BAC 1-11's, Tridents, Caravelles and Vanguards, Russian Ilyushins, Brittanias and VC 10's, as well as many other varied species including helicopters.

Although the main energies of the government have been directed towards the provision of modern airports and facilities for use by large size aeroplanes, landing strips to `

71

accommodate smaller aircraft have been contrasted in the Aran Islands, and a small feeder airline, Aer Arann, is successfully serving the community there for some time. Other remote areas are also being provided for, since no isolated population or small island is inaccessible to the modern flying machine. The ESB is acknowledged as having the most intensive network of rural electrification anywhere in the world, and it seems to me, that with the progress the state has made in aviation, it will only be a matter of time until there is a complete rural network of light aeroplane and helicopter communication throughout the country.

Irish industry has handsomely met its responsibility to aviation by intensive development work at the three major airports, ranking them in line with the finest in the world. The very large building at Shannon is geared for rapidly expanding traffic, and Dublin is a splendid example of airport architecture with a wide range of facilities and novel design features. Development at Cork has provided a new cargo terminal and a duty free shop.

The International Civil Aviation Organisation shares the expertise of airport construction, management and operation amongst its members. This worldwide assembly of nations fosters the common ground of all those who fly in aeroplanes, regularises the facilities, and establishes standards that are the result of long years of research, discussion and committee deliberation. Ireland has played an active part in ICAO by contributing to these advancements.

If at some future time you have to wait in the sunshine or the shadow at one of our fine Irish airports, perhaps you might think then of all the activity that throbs at the very heart of them. Think also of the men who built them, and in particular of one Irishman whose drive and energy led to their development.

At the airport of Dublin, a bronze plaque set in Wicklow granite commemorates him. The inscription reads:

IN MEMORY OF SEÁN LEMASS
WHOSE VISION, FORESIGHT
AND INITIATIVE
LED TO THE DEVELOPMENT OF THIS AIRPORT

CHAPTER SEVEN

THE AIRSPACE AND THE SEAS OF IRELAND

The waters and the air of this fair island
Unpolluted by the affairs of man,
Lie pure and untainted.
Go seek there thy pleasure.

In 1784 Mr Rosseau ascended in a balloon from Navan town—his companion on that memorable flight was a drummer boy only ten years old; this was the first manned flight into the enchanting colourful skies of Ireland. The bystanders had wished the aeronauts *bon voyage*, but none of them knew their destination, and neither did the balloonist himself; the height to which the primitive airship would rise, the speed of its flight and the duration were factors unknown even to Mr Rosseau.

Such indeed was the free-for-all situation existing in our airspace until the 1930s, when the nucleus of a control staff was formed by military officers on loan from the Air Corps. In 1943 a regular air traffic control service was organised under the guidance of Paddy Saul, who had been the navigator of the Southern Cross on its epic flight from Portmarnock Strand to North America in 1930. The majority of his staff, as might be expected, were ex-officers from Baldonnel.

In 1936 Aer Lingus began airline passenger schedules from the military base at Baldonnel, and the following year flying boats operated from the Shannon river at Foynes to Lisbon, West Africa, Southampton, the Azores, Botwood in

Newfoundland and on to New York. Later, landplanes from the adjacent airfield of Rineanna, now Shannon airport, provided a shuttle to and from England. All of these flights were handled by the embryo control service.

Aeroplanes have a fascination for everybody, but somehow the flying boat was the most appealing and majestic of them all. Here was the perfect blend of skill of sea and sky, because after the pilot had put the big plane down on the water, it might take him up to an hour to bring the craft to the anchorage, as he duelled with the winds and the tide. A burst of power from two engines on one side would prevent a wing tip from dipping into the water, but it could pirouette the boat and add to the difficulty of manoeuvring; in certain circumstances the aeroplane would have to be sailed to its refuge.

For a night take off at Foynes, a flare path of lighted guidance buoys had to be laid along the surface of the water. The control launch, with the markers attached to its stern, was always at the ready at the jetty, and when it chugged into the deep waters of the Shannon at dusk to position them, the ten little floats bobbed up and down behind them like ducks in a row.

The direction of the prevailing wind and the best stretch of the river was along the shipping lane, and there the flares were lowered into the water at intervals of 200 yards. As they were laid their lights were switched on—so the drill continued for a mile of the river.

Back at the anchorage near the jetty, the flying boat would be loading up. Last minute adjustments to the engines were carried out from platforms that were hinged down sections of the leading edge of the wing; tools or spare parts that were carelessly dropped fell straight down—into the Shannon.

Now the launch would have positioned itself at the upwind extremity of the take off run, but on the inactive side of the flare path. The flying boat lined up at the other end and the sound of its revving engines was accompanied by the aircraft captain's voice coming through the loud-speaker in the control launch: 'Ready for take off—release Flare Number One.'

The control officer jerked the lanyard of the mortar in the stern of the launch, and a parachute flare rocketed into the night; its brilliance flooded the whole area with an intense white light. In the distance the powerful propellers of the flying boat were now thrusting masses of spray behind them and labouring its heavy bulk through the clinging surface of the river; finally the waters receded from the bow and the huge craft planed across the Shannon on the step of the hull. Now, on a similar command, the second rocket replaced the dying light of its companion, and moments later the graceful machine was off the estuary and climbing slowly out towards the Atlantic.

The landing preparations were somewhat similar, but after a long ocean crossing, with unpredictable wind and limited nagivation aids, the actual arrival time of the big boat could be up to one hour later than the original estimate passed by radio. This meant a long cold stint for the launch—out at the flare path for an hour and a half before the arrival.

The machine homed into its landing run from radio bearings received from the radio station at Ballygireen, parachute flares were released as before, and the subsequent touch down was as spectacular as the take off.

Departures were generally at night, arrivals at dawn with some daylight operations. Although Foynes was remote from the war zone there was a risk of interception from German long range reconnaissance aircraft during those years—thus the protection of darkness was an added safety precaution.

The south-west coast of Ireland was on the patrol route of the Luftwaffe four engined Focke Wolfe Condors. One of these aircraft cut the corner off on its return flight and came to grief near Mount Brandon in Kerry; the Condor graunched slowly to a halt from full flight by coming into gradual and gentle contact with a slope on the mountain—

miraculously there were no casualities.

One arrival at Foynes caused considerable concern to the control staff: the aeroplane did not alight near the flare path and was nowhere to be seen; and although the control officer was certain that it was safely down, the radio bearings indicated its position to be on land.

The flying boat had in fact been short of fuel, and with bad weather and limited visibility at Foynes the pilot decided not to waste time and alighted on the first suitable water surface that he saw in the area—a tiny creek off the Shannon. The captain taxied the huge machine across to a fisherman and explained his predicament; the man abandoned his own little craft and went aboard the flying boat to guide it home up-river to Foynes.

Separation standards are now the very essence of aircraft safety, and they constitute the basic principles of air traffic control: aeroplanes are kept apart by height, speed, direction and time, or a combination of all four. Such methods were not fully developed in those early days, and an agitated air traffic officer at Foynes was handed over control responsibility by radio for two flying boats leaving the Canadian ocean sector.

The only snag with this normally routine business was that the two aeroplanes were flying at identical heights along a set route, and estimating similar positions at the same times. He radioed an urgent signal to one of the machines to change height, but his instructions were ignored—a further message was also disregarded. His fears were only allayed when a communication from the aircraft stated that the pilot had the other flying boat in sight since they had left Botwood, and that he was staying precisely where he was until they reached Foynes—a journey of nearly twelve hours!

During the years of the war, our non-military duties entailed manning the civil control tower at Dublin Airport; traffic was infrequent, and it was a simple but novel experience to be in charge of such a centre.

The instructions to the aircraft were relayed by wireless telegraphy, but the Lorenz Blind Landing System and the lighting facilities of the airfield were years ahead of their time.

If my flight commander was detailed for control duty, he arrived in a Gladiator fighter and beat the hell out of the place—drawing all the staff out to the airfield to enjoy a faultless display of barrel rolls and loops.

Greasing the biplane onto the grass, he would park in front of the terminal building, and then, casually undoing the straps of his parachute harness he would clamber down from the fighter and walk to the office: Crombie coat, Anthony Eden hat, rolled umbrella and morning newspaper.

From such romantic beginnings grew the Irish Air Traffic Control service, and through their disciplined skies flying machines are safely chaperoned. The Irish area of responsibility contains approximately 100,000 square miles of land and sea, and 46,000 feet of sky to go with it. The main control base is located at Shannon with subsidiary centres at Dublin and Cork.

Radar eyes plot and follow every mechanical object that moves in those skies; the system is called primary radar, with secondary radar as a refinement. International law requires each high flying aircraft to carry a transponder—that is where secondary radar comes in.

A transponder is a radio which is tuned by the pilot to a special frequency assigned by air traffic control. When the transponder is interrogated by the incoming radio beam, it triggers a reply burst on the ground operator's screen; further associated equipment on board the aircraft transmits its height.

The antenna of Shannon radar scans 200,000 square miles of sky, and it asks each aircraft in the region every ten seconds—Where are you now and what is your height? The information is fed to a computer bank where the individual signals from the various aircraft are translated into moving dots of light on a map; each radar dot is clearly labelled with the identification letters of the aircraft and its height. If an aeroplane is in distress, its dot pulsates brightly, and a bell rings in the control room.

This is the most sophisticated equipment in the world, with two additional stations to be introduced in Cork and Donegal to increase the efficiency of the system.

Two to three hundred aircraft traverse Irish airspace each day, and the radio conversations of the controllers and the pilots, together with any related telephone messages from the control tower, are recorded on tapes. The world-wide language of aviation is English, and the phrases have been standardised to remove any likelihood of misunderstanding.

In the midst of such stereotyped and refined control procedures the delightfully human intrudes from time to time—

'Cubana 934 requests permission to make an emergency landing at Shannon.' Shannon came back and queried: 'Cubana 934, what is the nature of your emergency?

The latin voice replied—'One of my passengers—she can not hold out any longer—she must to have her baby.' The baby was safely delivered in Ennis hospital, and the control officer was the god father.

The orderly progress of so many aeroplanes across our Irish skies is the result of well proven control techniques applied to airways; these are defined paths where entry points are marked by radio beacons from which aeroplanes can automatically deduce their own distances to the nearest mile. The flow of traffic along them is regulated by the separation methods; unfortunately in most countries, saturation does occur from time to time, but it can be eased out by requiring aircraft to orbit at an en route position before proceeding on course.

Saturation has become a major problem at most international airports: overseas flights tend to favour the same special time to arrive to connect with domestic networks, or with other carriers proceeding to far away destinations;

there are also choice times for the arrival and departure of internal flights, or for European inter city services.

When bad weather lends a hand to this tangle, it inhibits a continuous flow and forces aircraft to circle overhead for periods of up to one hour or more, or wait in long queues down below until they are assigned a slot in the departure sequence. I used to know one area, where a case of Irish whiskey, delivered at Christmas with the compliments of the pilots to the controllers, produced amazing results when the fuel was low on an Irish aeroplane.

*   *   *

Although these pure skies and untainted waters lie inviting for the benefit of man, they also require a custodian to supervise his activities, and so a Marine Rescue Co-ordination Centre is located at Shannon, and the responsibility for its operation is vested in the air traffic control authorities. The purpose of the rescue centre is to provide a central command structure which can rapidly organise effective and speedy assistance to any distress at sea. The general area in which this service is given extends to approximately 100 nautical miles from the Irish coastline, since this distance is within the range of the Irish land-based Search and Rescue—SAR helicopters, and the light coastal aircraft of the Irish Army Air Corps.

In the Irish Sea and the south coastal area, emergency services are the joint responsibility of the Irish and British SAR centres. At distances in excess of 100 nautical miles from the coast, help is provided by ships in the immediate vicinity, and by long range British Nimrod jet aircraft; this machine has an immense radius of action, and it is equipped with the most comprehensive search and detection gear. Piston engined Shackletons, together with the Nimrods, provide safety cover for Air Corps SAR helicopters when operating at abnormal distances from the shoreline.

The facilities and the help available to the service come from the following sources:

Lifeboats around the coastline, together with some inshore boats;

Coast Watching Stations;

Air Corps helicopters and light coastal search aeroplanes;

Irish naval units;

Liaison United Kingdom Aeronautical Rescue Co-ordination Centres, and in addition, their coastguard and coast radio stations;

The American Automated Mutual-Assistance Vessel Rescue System;

Maritime Garda stations;

Irish lighthouses and light vessels;

Irish port harbour authorities;

Shipping or aircraft in the vicinity of the casualty area;

Ships in harbour;

Radio Telefís Éireann, and occasionally telephone operators, seaside hotels and local bars.

The American Automated Mutual-Assistance Vessel Rescue System is a computer bank operated by the United States Coastguard; the name, position and speed of every ship sailing the North Atlantic is retained in its electronic brain. Within minutes of any mishap at sea, the Shannon controller can obtain from the system details of all shipping in the proximity of the distress area.

This diverse group is knitted tightly together by telephone, teleprinter and radio, and all of the messages which they originate, and each of the duty officer's decisions or actions are carefully logged in the operations diary at the centre. The watch is manned day and night, and a meteorologist is always available to provide weather information for the sea areas—actual sea conditions are supplied by shipping, lighthouses, lifeboats or coastal stations.

When the controller is advised of an emergency at sea, he identifies the position on a marine chart, and then from the information available to him he will normally be able to direct a ship to the distress area. His assessment of the situation will determine what other help is necessary: in some instances a doctor may have to be flown out to a vessel, or an injured seaman airlifted to hospital.

All of life is present in the diaries: tragedy, human error, crises, heroism and unselfishness, together with the spontaneous off-the-cuff humour of the many Irishmen involved: humour that lightens the burden for the distressed and stimulates the efforts of the rescuers.

'3 March 1973.

Lifeboat station at Howth phoned with information that UK vessel ——, outward bound from Dublin to the USA, has an injured crewman on board, and requested helicopter assistance to bring the casualty to hospital. It was arranged that Air Corps helicopter would leave at first light. . .'

Before the helicopter left Baldonnel the ship signalled to say that they had discovered a stowaway—a woman, and requested that she would be transported back to Dublin. Now the usual difficult problem arose—the nationality of the girl; as far as the centre knew, the lady was Irish but there was a doubt. The indecisive silence at the military end of the telephone was finally broken when the chopper pilot's voice said: 'Well f— the begrudgers—I'll take her anyway.'

'31 April 1973.

This was an extremely busy day, with 3 incidents going on simultaneously:

Helicopter overdue enroute Bournemouth to Cork.

Garda at Easkey reported 3 surf-riders appear to be drifting out to sea.

Aircraft overdue on flight to Keflavik, Iceland.'

All ended well: the chopper made a forced landing at Waterford; an Air Corps helicopter picked up the surfers after a 20 minute search in deteriorating weather, and the overdue aircraft landed safely in Iceland.

'*1 September 1973.*

German ship *Elbemarchen* on rocks off Cliffs of Moher.
Rescue co-ordination had begun late on 31 August.
Weather in area of ship—WSW Force 8, visibility 1½ miles.
Squalls, drizzle and heavy seas. . .'

The staff of the Coast Life Saving Service, with ten local
men descended 300 feet to the ship and took off six of the
crew, placing them on a ledge to be picked up by a Royal
Navy Seaking rescue helicopter. The chopper had just flown
back from the dramatic search for the deep diving mini sub-
marine *Pisces III.*

'*13 October 1973.*

Panamanian vessel *Dani*—engine room on fire. Position 2
miles west of Inish Tearagh—needs immediate assistance.

Valentia lifeboat launched, and naval vessel *Deirdre*
within 30 minutes, and proceeding towards *Dani.'*

'*24 March 1974.*

Coastguard Landsend reported to MRCC that Russian
factory ship *Kazan* in position 60 miles south of the Blaskets had crewman very ill, and requested helicopter lift-off
to hospital.'

Diplomatic clearance was obtained for the use of the
helicopter, but the lift-off could not be made as the *Kazan*
was moving too fast and would not reduce speed; its stern
was a mass of ropes and masts and there was a heavy swell.
The patient had to be taken off by the Limerick pilot boat.

'*14 April 1974.*

Ennistymon Garda Siochána phoned to say: "New currach stolen by hippies. Capability of thieves as seamen
doubtful. Craft observed drifting near Cliffs of Moher."

Valentia lifeboat located the currach and towed it to
safety. The lifeboat got back to its station after seven hours
of hard work.

'24 April 1974.

Coast Radio Station Valentia linked up skipper of Irish fishing vessel with MRCC at 1755 hours; skipper complained strongly of three Norwegian shark fishing vessels operating in Bantry Bay, just ½ mile off shore. Norwegians just taking fish livers and throwing back carcasses—at it several days now—what are we, MRCC, going to do about it?

Explained to skipper that all we could do was to pass the information on to the Naval Service; this did not mollify him, and salty opinions on ancestry of Norwegians offered.'

It later turned out that the intruders were Bulgarian.

'11 June 1974.

Aer Lingus flight inbound to Dublin reported "oil slick NE of the Baily". This was the lighter *Shamrock II* dumping her usual cargo!'

'21 August 1974.

From Coastal Radio Station Valentia at 0406 hours—"Spanish fishing vessel *Cabo Villano*—170 miles west of Blaskets, crew member severly injured, leg hanging off—request helicopter assistance. Heading Valentia, speed 9 knots."

Air Corps Casement alerted and helicopter on standby for dawn departure. Southern Rescue Co-ordination Centre contacted with details and air cover requested and approved. Lifeboat station at Valentia informed and lifeboat launched at 0500 hours—intercept course determined and passed to lifeboat through Coastal Radio Station. Doctor arranged to travel with helicopter. All weather information obtained and passed to lifeboat, helicopter and Nimrod: usual liaison with air traffic control. Nimrod located fishing vessel about 105 miles off coast, and when the vessel came to 60 miles, helicopter performed lift-off. Patient arrived Tralee hospital 1230 hours. Lifeboat returned to station 1630 hours.'

'1 September 1974.
Usual queries on yachts—one overdue at Dun Laoghaire had never left Crosshaven.'

'14 October 1974.
District Officer, Coastguard Bangor phoned to report that "a clairvoyant phoned Bangor twice from London that he 'saw' a boat numbered—on a rocky shore near a lighthouse in difficulty."

Bangor suggested that we check out the "vision". Bord Iascaigh Mhara supplied the information that —— was registered jointly by two fishermen from —— near Fenit. Fenit has a lighthouse. A phone call confirmed the owners and the boat safe and well. The owners called the MRCC later in the day as to why their boat was of interest to MRCC, and were not too pleased when given above details. MRCC put them in touch with Bangor, as they wanted to know the name of the clairvoyant.'

The rescue officers at the Shannon MRCC are air traffic controllers who have been trained to standards that equip them to deal with marine problems. They share their experiences with their international colleagues and are justifiably proud of their contribution to the safety of all those who use the airspace and the seas of Ireland.

CHAPTER EIGHT

TOMORROW

Clip no feather from an eagle's wing,
Limit not the creature's meaning,
Whose purpose evolved from ageless time
And evolves in ageless meaning.

Long haul passengers ships, except for holiday cruising, have almost disappeared from the oceans of the earth, and although heavy freight is still transported by sea, the cargo aeroplane has made huge inroads into the shipping business. Natural produce too is a natural flyer, and is almost totally carried by air. It requires little special packaging or attention in transit, and it is flown directly from producer to consumer: mushrooms from Dublin, pineapples from Nairobi, tulips from Amsterdam, beef to Libya and lamb to Paris. Processed textiles as well as horses, sheep and dairy products—all take to wings with remarkable ease.

When in 1971, the first jumbo was introduced by the Boeing Airplane Company, it was followed closely by other manufacturers with their different models of wide-bodied jets: Douglas with the three-engined DC 10, Lockheed the 1011 Tristar, and the French have the very successful and economical European Airbus. A wide-bodied aeroplane is broad in the beam, and the concept has proved to be very popular with the passenger, conveying an air of spaciousness far removed from the claustrophobic tube-like cabins of early planes.

An eminent English aeronautical engineer of some years

ago, considered that the passenger aeroplane of the future would be a relatively small capacity jet, flying just below the speed of sound at a very high altitude. He envisaged large numbers of such planes would provide the answer to frequency and speed; but then, he could not have foreseen the congestion that they would have caused at the major airports: serious overcrowding existed in the airspace over large cities and on the airfields beneath, prior to the introduction of the big capacity jets.

Today, there is every indication that for long and short-haul work, the high density large aeroplane will cater for the worldwide travel needs of tourist passengers for many years to come; the big jets will be augmented by a variety of smaller machines, when frequency and not capacity is the requirement.

Very soon too, first class travel will be provided exclusively by supersonic planes, flying at extreme heights above the earth's surface. The French-British Concorde, and the Russian TU 144 are the first generation of these faster-than-sound passenger jets, but yet they are only half the size of the Boeing 747, and with an average seating capacity of 120.

Traditionally, the marriage between the aero engine and the design structure of the actual body of the craft was not a happy one. Aeroplane builders had always complained that the engine manufacturers could not provide them with adequate power to propel their aircraft; but, with the arrival of the jet engine the trend reversed: these new engines were capable of pushing the flying machine to velocities where the phenomena of flight control behaviour at or near the speed of sound was not fully understood. Problems also arose in devising materials which were light but strong enough to withstand the stresses of such fast speeds; these difficulties were overcome by the metallurgists, who invented many new materials with the capability of resisting very high temperatures and loads.

Nevertheless, the supersonic era created further and different obstacles for the designer. In theory at least, on the

87

basis of present engine design and projected development, there is almost no limit to the amount of thrust such a power plant can be made to deliver, but there are penalties for having these large engines. The carriage of enormous quantities of fuel to supply them, bearing in mind that almost a quarter of that same fuel has to be consumed to carry itself; air flow problems in incorporating such large engines in a streamlined body, and environmental pollution from noise and fuel deposits.

Larger jumbo capacity supersonic airliners will be built when smaller engines are available, which will produce greater thrust from a lightweight fuel that occupies less volume. Meanwhile, in complete contrast, interest has been renewed in slow flying big airships, capable of transporting large passenger and cargo loads, inexpensively over long distances.

Our old romantic friend, the commercial flying boat has long since disappeared, but amphibians—a combined land and sea aeroplane—floatplanes and small flying boats will always be required for operations from water surfaces. The helicopter has become the ubiquitous workhorse of everyman, uplifting passengers or massive loads and transporting them to places hitherto inaccessible. Its speed and range capability have increased considerably, and it may well be that it will replace the conventional aeroplane for inter city travel; no precious land is required for its exclusive patronage, and it is equally at home in any geographic location or inhospitable surface.

It is inevitable that wingless rocket propelled machines will encompass the earth in the next century, or perhaps even earlier, and also that travel agents will be able to offer all-in weekends in exotic hotels at choice locations on the moon; alternatively, ten day cruises in inner or outer space will be as common as a boat tour on the Shannon.

In our reality of aviation in Ireland, fast modern aeroplanes are transporting passengers and cargo, around the clock, to the ends of the earth. The reliability of these aeroplanes of our day is the result of their design features, where systems are either duplicated or triplicated, components are readily accessible, and the engines are the ultimate in the delivery of smooth uninterrupted power.

Now that you know all about those fine Irish airports that play host to the jumbos and their many companions from around the world, let us praise the thousands of men and women of Ireland who provide us with such an excellent aviation service.

May the sky rise up to meet you too, Patrick Loueiro, because you were born to a Portugese passenger at 15,000 feet in one of our jumbos on 11 June 1975. The aeroplane was flying over Zambia—just west of Lusaka when the little boy arrived; during his first days of life he flew almost 7,000 miles.

To you, kind reader, may I plagiarise an old Irish blessing and wish:

> 'Land without rent to you,
> Aeroplanes galore to you
> And, may you fly in Ireland.'

THE BOOK OF IRISH CURSES
By Patrick C. Power

The Book of Irish Curses is an extremely interesting, well written, fascinating and entertaining book. It is a remarkable blend of history, forklore and anecdote. The author deals at length with the types of Irish curses, their age and styles, their rituals, and concludes with a do-it-yourself cursing kit.

IN MY FATHER'S TIME
By Eamon Kelly

In My Father's Time invites us to a night of storytelling by Ireland's greatest and best loved *seanchaí*, Eamon Kelly. The fascinating stories reveal many aspects of Irish life and character. There are tales of country customs; matchmaking, courting, love; marriage and the dowry system; emigration, American wakes and returned emigrants. The stream of anecdotes never runs dry and the humour sparkles and illuminates the stories.

FABLES AND LEGENDS OF IRELAND
By Maureen Donegan

These tales were told and retold by word of mouth and, although they are full of magical creatures and enchanted castles, they are also about people: real people who suffered from indigestion and jealousy, just as we do. The Fianna, larger than life and swashbuckling across Ireland even into fairy cities beyond the sea, still live on, in spirit if not in the flesh, in an Ireland which is much changed since giants and heroes strode across it.

THE FIRST BOOK OF IRISH MYTHS AND LEGENDS
By Eoin Neeson

THE SECOND BOOK OF IRISH MYTHS AND LEGENDS
By Eoin Neeson

These two books contain a fascinating collection of tales and legends of Irish heroes.

IRISH COUNTRY PEOPLE
Kevin Danaher

Irish Country People is simply one fascinating glorious feast of folklore and interesting sidelights of history recorded without a fraction of a false note or a grain of sentimentality. The topics covered in the twenty essays range over a wide field of history, folklore, mythology and archaeology. There are discussions about cures, curses and charms; lords, labourers and wakes; names, games and ghosts; prayers and fairy-tales. Nowadays we find it hard to visualise the dark winter evenings of those times when there was no electric light, radio, television or cinemas. We find it harder to realise that such evenings were not usually long enough for the games, singing, card-playing, music, dancing and story-telling that went on.

We can read about a six-mile traffic jam near Tailteann in the year 1168, just before the Norman invasion, and the incident is authenticated by a reference to the *Annals of the Four Masters*. The whole book is tinged with quiet humour: 'You should always talk to a dog in a friendly, mannerly way, but you should never ask him a question directly, for what would you do if he answered you, as well he might?'

THE PLEASANT LAND OF IRELAND
Kevin Danaher

This book is well illustrated and gives a comprehensive picture of a way of life which though in great part is vanishing is still familiar to many of our countrymen.

LETTERS OF A SUCCESSFUL T.D.

This bestseller takes a humourous peep at the correspondence of an Irish parliamentary deputy. Keane's eyes have fastened on the human weaknesses of a man who secured power through the ballot box, and uses it to ensure the comfort of his family and friends.

LETTERS OF AN IRISH PARISH PRIEST

There is a riot of laughter in every page and its theme is the correspondence between a country parish priest and his nephew who is studying to be a priest. Father O'Mora has been referred to by one of his parishioners as one who 'is suffering from an overdose of racial memory aggravated by religious bigotry.' John B. Keane's humour is neatly pointed, racy of the soil and never forced. This book gives a picture of a way of life which though in great part is vanishing is still familiar to many of our countrymen who still believe 'that priests could turn them into goats.' It brings out all the humour and pathos of Irish life. It is hilariously funny and will entertain and amuse everyone.

LETTERS OF A LOVE-HUNGRY FARMER

John B. Keane has introduced a new word into the English language — *chastitute*. This is the story of a chastitute, i.e. a man who has never lain down with a woman for reasons which are fully disclosed within this book. It is the tale of a lonely man who will not humble himself to achieve his heart's desire, whose need for female companionship whines and whimpers throughout. Here are the hilarious sex escapades of John Bosco McLane culminating finally in one dreadful deed.

LETTERS OF AN IRISH PUBLICAN

In this book we get a complete picture of life in Knockanee as seen through the eyes of a publican, Martin MacMeer. He relates his story to his friend Dan Stack who is a journalist. He records in a frank and factual way events like the cattle fair where the people 'came in from the hinterland with caps and ash-plants and long coats', and the cattle stood 'outside the doors of the houses in the public streets'. Through his remarkable perception we 'get a tooth' for all the different characters whom he portrays with sympathy, understanding and wit. We are overwhelmed by the charms of the place where at times 'trivial incidents assume new proportions.' These incidents are exciting, gripping, hilarious, touching and uncomfortable.

THE GENTLE ART OF MATCHMAKING
and other important things

This book offers a feast of Keane, one of Ireland's best loved playwrights. The title essay reminds us that while some marriages are proverbially made in heaven, others have been made in the back parlour of a celebrated pub in Listowel and none the worse for that! But John B. Keane has other interests besides matchmaking, and these pieces mirror many moods and attitudes. Who could ignore Keane on Potato-Cakes? Keane on skinless sausages? or Half-Doors? Is there a husband alive who will not recognise someone near and dear to him when he reads, with a mixture of affection and horror, the essay 'Female Painters'? And, more seriously, there are other pieces that reflect this writer's deep love of tradition: his nostalgic re-creation of an Irish way of life that is gone forever.

LOVE POEMS OF THE IRISH
Edited by Sean Lucy

This anthology shows those people who seem to think that we are a loveless race, how wrong they are. It takes a wide view of what can be called love poetry, a view which embraces a whole landscape of feeling between men and women as men and women, and does not confine itself to poems about being 'in love' in the more restricted meaning of that term.

THE TAILOR AND ANSTY
Eric Cross

The tailor and his wife lived in Co Cork, yet the width of the world could barely contain his wealth of humour and fantasy. Marriages, inquests, matchmaking — everything is here.

THE FARM BY LOUGH GUR
Mary Carbery

This is the true story of a family who lived on a farm by Lough Gur, the Enchanted Lake, in Co Limerick. Their home, shut away from the turmoil of politics, secure from apprehension of unemployment and want, was a world in itself. The master with his men, the mistress with her maids worked in happy unity. The four little girls, growing up in this contented atmosphere, dreamed of saints and fairies. The story is also a picture of manners and customs in a place so remote that religion had still to reckon with pagan survivals, where a fairy-doctor cured the landlord's bewitched cows, and a banshee comforted the dying with the music of harps and flutes.